The Urban Girl's Manifesto

Melody Biringer

The Urban Girl's Manifesto

We CRAVE Community.
At CRAVE Chicago we believe in acknowledging, celebrating, and passionately supporting local businesses. We know that, when encouraged to thrive, neighborhood establishments enhance communities and provide rich experiences not usually encountered in mass-market. We hope that, by introducing you to the savvy business women in this guide, CRAVE Chicago will help inspire your own inner entrepreneur.

We CRAVE Adventure.
We could all use a getaway, and at CRAVE Chicago we believe that you don't need to be a jet setter to have a little adventure. There's so much to do and to explore right in your own backyard. We encourage you to break your routine, to venture away from your regular haunts, to visit new businesses, to explore all the funky finds and surprising spots that Chicago has to offer. Whether it's to hunt for a birthday gift, indulge in a spa treatment, order a bouquet of flowers, or connect with like-minded people, let CRAVE Chicago be your guide for a one-of-a-kind hometown adventure.

We CRAVE Quality.
CRAVE Chicago is all about quality products and thoughtful service. We know that a satisfying shopping trip requires more than a simple exchange of money for goods, and that a rejuvenating spa date entails more than a quick clip of the cuticles and a swipe of polish. We know you want to come away feeling uplifted, beautiful, excited, relaxed, relieved and, above all, knowing you got the most bang for your buck. We have scoured the city to find the hidden gems, new hot spots, and old standbys, all with one thing in common: they're the best of the best!

A Guide to our Guide

CRAVE Chicago is more than a guidebook. It's a savvy, quality-of-lifestyle book devoted entirely to the best local businesses owned by women. CRAVE Chicago will direct you to over 100 local spots—top boutiques, spas, cafes, stylists, fitness studios, and more. And we'll introduce you to the inspired, dedicated women behind these exceptional enterprises, for whom creativity, quality, innovation, and customer service are paramount. Not only is CRAVE Chicago an intelligent guidebook for those wanting to know what's happening throughout town, it's a directory for those who value the contributions that spirited businesswomen make to our city.

Consumer Business Section
Consumer-driven entreprenesses, including boutiques, spas, and food.

Intelligentsia Directory
Business-to-Business entreprenesses, including coaching, marketing and public relations, photography, business consulting, and design services.

CRAVE Categories
ABODE - Home/interior design related.
ADORN - Jewelry-related boutiques, goods, and services.
CHILDREN'S - Baby, children, and mom-related products and services.
CONNECT - Networking, media, technology, and event services.
DETAILS - Miscellaneous goods and services.
ENHANCE - Spa, salon, and beauty, fitness studios and trainers.
PETS - Pet-related services.
SIP SAVOR - Food, drink, and caterers.
STYLE - Clothing boutiques, shoes, eyewear, handbags, stylists, etc.

Who is your role model or mentor?

"*Madonna. She's ever-evolving, surprising, gutsy, and a successful business woman*"

Lauren Lein of Lauren Lein Ltd.

Julia Archer

 Q and A

What are your most popular products or services?
The home office accessories, such as LED task lighting, organization accessories, and seating.

People may be surprised to know...
We offer not just new lines of furnishings but we also provide lifestyle products, such as felt slippers or coats made of Tyvek. We also use vintage product solutions to bring an eclectic style to our offering.

What or who inspired you to start your business?
I have always been inspired by good design, and with my background as a creative director for various corporate and design organizations, creating a retail business became a way to reinvent and apply my interests and passions.

What is your indulgence?
Cappuccinos and *The New York Times*.

Where is your favorite place to go with your girlfriends?
Coffeehouse/café destinations.

@WORKDESIGN

7500 W Madison St, Forest Park, 708.488.9297
atworkdesign.com, Twitter: @atworkdesign

Stylish. Functional. Modern.
@WorkDesign is a new specialty retail store that is bringing stylish, functional and hard-to-get home office furnishings and accessories to the Chicago area from the world's most innovative designers. @WorkDesign offers a wide range of high-quality, design-driven, yet affordable work-space product solutions from desks, seating, and other furnishings to lighting, shelving, paper goods, and computer bags. We are the complete one-stop resource for people who want to seamlessly integrate their work and life, and who believe that great design is a lifestyle essential.

1154 LILL STUDIO

904 W Armitage Ave, Chicago, 773.477.5455
1154LILL.com, Twitter: @LILL_DesignTeam, facebook.com/1154LILLStudio

Creative. Collaborative. Customizable.
1154 LILL STUDIO is the original custom handbag boutique where you mix and match fabrics and styles to design a one-of-a-kind bag. Established in Chicago in 1999 and currently operating in Chicago, Boston, and Kansas City boutiques, 1154 LILL STUDIO also has a nationwide handbag party program, as well as a dynamic Web site at 1154LILL.com.

Jennifer Velarde

Q and A

People may be surprised to know...
I didn't have enough product to sell at my first event, so I took custom orders. Customers loved it, and a niche was born!

What or who inspired you to start your business?
My job at the time was unfulfilling. I was looking for something I could personally connect with and make a living doing.

Who is your role model or mentor?
My husband is also an entrepreneur. He shows me that anything is possible if you view it with the right perspective.

What business mistake have you made that you will not repeat?
Standing still is not an option. You must always be considering what is next.

What is your indulgence?
An uninterrupted afternoon alone with my sewing machine.

Q and A

Trudy Robinson Foley with her son, Keaney

What are your most popular products or services?
Kickin': versatile black dresses that can be worn five different ways, designer maternity jeans, custom necklaces with baby names, and slings. At À Pied: mid-height heels that are artistic, yet affordable, and high-heeled water-proof boots for the Chicago winters.

What or who inspired you to start your business?
My sister Darcy's pregnancy and my previous job as a magazine publisher for the same company that owned Fit Pregnancy magazine.

Who is your role model or mentor?
My mom for being a strong business woman, and my dad for his entrepreneurial spirit.

What business mistake have you made that you will not repeat?
Being closed on Mondays. You never know what day will be a good day. We'll always try to be open all days.

How do you spend your free time?
Engaging in active endeavors such as sailing, skiing, and traveling with my husband.

Kickin'

Kickin'

À Pied

À PIED

2037 W Roscoe St, Chicago, 773.281.2210
apiedshoeboutique.com

KICKIN'

2142 W Roscoe St, Chicago, 773.281.6577
kickinmaternity.com

Fresh. Approachable. Fashionable.
In 2006, Trudy opened Kickin'—an active boutique for moms-to-be and babes. The boutique is known for great maternity fashion from formal to activewear, as well as nursing and baby apparel. Within two years she decided that Roscoe Village needed another boutique, this time one that would help women's feet look beautiful while feeling comfortable. At À Pied ("on foot" in French) discover shoes that are ready for a busy day of shopping in the neighborhood or dancing the night away downtown.

ABOUT FACE COSMETICS

404 W Fifth Ave, Naperville, 630.369.5770
theshespace.com, Twitter: @theshespace

Edgy. Customized. Affordable.
About Face Cosmetics is a local, unique product line created and manufactured in Naperville.
With products currently worn by women across the globe, About Face offers everything from
customized eye shadows and foundations, to ready-to-wear products, featuring over 300
eye colors for the true color junkie! Products are available both in-store and online.

Heather Hanson

 Q and A

What are your most popular products or services?
By far our customized cosmetics—eyeshadows, blush, foundations, and lip balms.

People may be surprised to know...
A locally manufactured cosmetics line can truly stand up to the department store brands—without the high price tag.

Who is your role model or mentor?
Betsy Johnson and Liz Claiborne.

What business mistake have you made that you will not repeat?
Trying to please everybody instead of following my instincts.

What is your indulgence?
Shoes and handbags.

Where is your favorite place to go with your girlfriends?
A night at home with a bottle of wine (or three!) and good conversation.

Adele Dallas Orr

Q and A

What are your most popular products or services?
Reversible silk jackets, ruffle silk coats, wearable art silk skirts and scarves, and statement jewelry made with faceted black onyx and fresh-water pearls.

What or who inspired you to start your business?
My love of fashion and travel and the will to work for myself. I also perceived a niche in the market to design elegant European-styled clothes for women of all ages, at an accessible price.

Who is your role model or mentor?
My role model is Coco Chanel, who believed that women should be two things: classy and fabulous. I always design with these wise words in mind.

How do you spend your free time?
I read fashion and travel magazines published in various languages—I speak and read five languages. The magazines keep me informed of current trends everywhere, and they're a fun way to practice my language skills.

ADELE DALLAS ORR PRET A PORTER BOUTIQUE

520 N Michigan Ave, Level 3, Chicago, 312.755.0011
adeledallasorr.com

Classy. Fabulous. Stylish.

Adele Dallas Orr designs her unique, colorful fashion collection with class in mind. Her boutique carries separates and fashion jewelry that reflect her love of color, exotic prints, and silky textures, inspired by her travels to South Africa, Europe, and Asia. Adele's versatile pieces are easily accessorized with her exquisite jewelry, made of fresh-water pearls and semi-precious stones. Her stylish, timeless clothing and accessories have a European flair for women of all ages and are ideal for Chicago's stylish woman.

ANIKO SALON AND SPA

1109 S Wabash Ave, Chicago, 312.431.1573
anikosalonspa.com, Twitter: @anikosalonspa, facebook.com/anikosalonspa

Blissful. Escape. Couture.
Aniko Salon and Spa is a family-operated full-service salon and spa offering hair design, massages, facials, and hand, foot, and body treatments. Aniko was voted No. 1 Salon and Spa in the South Loop by Yelp in 2009. Aniko's attention to detail and superior customer service keep clients coming back for more.

Marti Goyal

Q and A

What are your most popular products or services?
Services: Aniko massage, spa facial, and our famous haute haircuts. Products: Redken hair care and Bioelements skin care.

What or who inspired you to start your business?
I was brought up in an entrepreneurial environment. It's always been a passion of mine to run my own business.

Who is your role model or mentor?
My mother has provided me with guidance and support to run my own business, and to become an effective leader.

How do you spend your free time?
I spend my free time with my family and friends, attending social events, giving back to the community, and traveling.

What is your indulgence?
I love cupcakes and Tory Burch sandals!

custom
LETTERPRESS

Kristie Lee Wagner

Q and A

What are your most popular products or services?
By far the custom wedding invitations we create by hand—from couture boxes with live orchids to elegant folios adorned with Swarovski crystals.

People may be surprised to know...
Our invitations can be letterpressed in soy ink, on handmade paper embedded with sweet basil seeds that your guests can grow in their garden.

What or who inspired you to start your business?
I've had many ideas and ambitions, and have changed jobs more often than outfits! One dream always remained—someday I would own a boutique. I combined my fabulous card-making skills with an entrepreneurial fascination, and Anjénu was born!

Who is your role model or mentor?
My husband, Shawn. He has been there every step of the way and is the most caring and thoughtful person I've ever known. He continually inspires me.

ANJÉNU

1747 W Division St, Chicago, 773.469.2212
anjenu.com

Charming. Bright. Inspiring.
Anjénu is Wicker Park's exclusive paper boutique, with bamboo-green walls and a charming personality.
Offering handmade greetings, stationery, and vibrant papers, owner Kristie Lee Wagner strives to revive
the love of a handwritten note. So next time you need the perfect card, swing by for a unique paper
experience. And don't forget to say hello to the store's mascot, Molasses, the adorable mini dachshund.

ARTHUR MURRAY DANCE CENTERS

116 W Illinois St., Chicago, 312.644.7554
chicagoarthurmurray.com

Fun. Cool. Rewarding.
Arthur Murray is the world's premier dance studio, teaching the finest in ballroom, Latin, swing, and salsa! Whether you're single, a couple, beginner, or advanced, we can help you spice up your life by learning to dance at any of our five Chicago locations! Perfect for exercise, stress relief, meeting people, or getting ready for a special occasion—being a great dancer never goes out of STYLE!

Q and A

Jill DeMarlo

What are your most popular products or services?
Private lessons whenever it's convenient,
salsa, swing, and Tango classes, dance events,
competitions, wedding classes, night out parties.

People may be surprised to know...
Anyone can learn to dance! And you could go out
dancing every night of the week if you so desired!

What or who inspired you to start your business?
I thought it would be fun to teach ballroom dancing
through college. Once I saw what an impact
dancing had on so many people, I couldn't stop!

Who is your role model or mentor?
Arthur Murray himself was not only a great dancer, but
a brilliant business man. I feel fortunate to combine
a great business with my passion for dancing!

What business mistake have you made
that you will not repeat?
Listening to people who are afraid. It's easy to
buy in to naysayers; but do what you love with
passion and success will surely follow!

Christine Adar Ammon

Q and A

What are your most popular products or services?
The online storefront for independent designers in fashion, art, and furniture. Buy, sell, and network in one place.

People may be surprised to know...
We give a portion of our profits directly to charity.

What or who inspired you to start your business?
Hard-working, extremely talented, and undiscovered designers and artists.

What business mistake have you made that you will not repeat?
Not trusting my gut instincts about the people you choose to do business with.

What is your indulgence?
Shoes, extravagant fabrics, and dark chocolate.

Where is your favorite place to go with your girlfriends?
The spa!

Help | Register | Sign In

🛒 View Cart

Search

HOME   SHOWROOM   DESIGNERS   MEMBERS   INDUSTRY RESOURCES   JOBS   ABOUT US

Summer 2009
Electric city

Summer '09 Look Book

Shop Summer Fashions

What's New

News & Events

TUESDAY, MAY 5

Summer 2009 Trends to Watch

Bright colors are it for summer. Look for sunny yellows, bright tangerine and bold lime. [more]

FRIDAY, MAY 1

Built By Wendy Sample Sale

Get great items from a fabulous designer at prices you'll love. [more]

THURSDAY, APRIL 30

Style Tips

Here is an interview from Sarah James, Assistant Fashion Editor at Lucky. Read her answers to all your fashion questions. [more]

View all news and events

Featured Designer

AngelRox

After making its debut in 2007 AngelRox has been busy creating timeless looks in easy to wear fabrics.

Go to shop

Forum

Help designers & shoppers with your ideas.

MOST RECENT TOPICS

What to wear to an outdoor wedding? 12 responses

Does this outfit work? 36 responses

What should I wear to an interview? 10 responses

View all discussions

Home x Showroom x Designers x Members x Industry Resources x Jobs x About Us x Help x Terms

B4UCIT

Chicago, 608.295.5192
b4ucit.com

Fashion-forward. Trendsetting. Innovative.

B4UCIT is a unique and exciting new concept—an online storefront for independent designers in fashion, art, and furniture. B4UCIT's Web site is a place for creative designers to reach the broadest customer base, with the least amount of investment, and a place for customers with discerning tastes to find unique pieces. With B4UCIT you can buy, sell, and network all in one place.

BACKBEAT MUSIC INSTRUCTION

1519 W Irving Park, Chicago, 773.256.9475
backbeatmusic.net, Twitter: @musicalmoxie

Spirited. Sharing. Inspiring.
With a goal to teach, inspire, and promote an understanding of, and passion for, music,
BackBeat offers personalized music lessons and classes to students of all ages. Founded
in 2007 by Meghan Hormann, BackBeat has grown dramatically in a mere two years,
thanks to her passion for music and enthusiasm for sharing it with the community.

Meghan Hormann

 Q and A

What are your most popular products or services?
Piano lessons and KinderChoir.

People may be surprised to know...
I'm only 25 years old. They hear me on the phone and tend to be surprised when they meet me in person.

What or who inspired you to start your business?
A bad job experience. I was hurt when I left, then I realized it was a golden opportunity to do it better.

Who is your role model or mentor?
My Aunt Cathy. I always saw her bucking the trends, so I just assumed that was the norm.

How do you spend your free time?
Tasting new wines with my roommates, dwelling on new business ideas, reading business books, or biking in Chicago

What is your indulgence?
Coffee and my iPhone. I love to go to Asado Coffee, right by the studio, and answer e-mails.

BARKER & MEOWSKY, A PAW FIRM

1003 W Armitage Ave, Chicago, 773.868.0200
barkerandmeowsky.com, Twitter: @barker_meowsky, facebook.com/barkerandmeowsky

Fun. Knowledgeable. Stylish.
Barker & Meowsky has been celebrating and promoting the bond between people and their pets for over a decade. Their love for their own furry friends drives their commitment to products that embody the best in safety, quality, and style. Barker & Meowsky is proud to be Chicago's premier pet boutique, having been featured in national and international television and print.

Alice Lerman

Q and A

What are your most popular products or services?
Expert, caring, grooming services, and an unrivaled selection of stylish collars, comfy beds, fashionable coats, sweaters, and much more.

People may be surprised to know...
We have an on-site tailor to ensure that your dog's outerwear fits perfectly!

What or who inspired you to start your business?
Woody and Boris, my first dog and cat, were in dire need of better wardrobes, healthier foods, as well as beds and bowls that I didn't want to hide when friends came over.

Who is your role model or mentor?
My dad has been both my role model and my mentor through his example of hard work, business ethics, integrity, and creativity.

What is your indulgence?
I love Pilates!

Eden Novak DeGenova

 Q and A

What are your most popular products or services?
I provide a full range of lingerie, as well as expert bra-fitting services. O Lingerie and 68 are two exclusive lines we carry that have been very successful.

Who is your role model or mentor?
Any woman who continues to reinvent herself.

How do you spend your free time?
I perform as an actress and musician. I garden, roller skate, write, and continually generate new ideas to expand my business and keep it fresh for myself and for my customers.

What is your indulgence?
I *love* horseback riding and try to spend one week every year riding in a different locale.

Where is your favorite place to go with your girlfriends?
After roller derby practice, we head to a local restaurant for margaritas and nachos. Or there is a tiny bar by the Brookfield Zoo with great martinis called The Blue Water Lounge.

BAUBO'S GARDEN

7234 W Madison, Forest Park, 708.771.8900
baubosgarden.com, Twitter: @baubosgarden

Sophisticated. Sexy. Fun.
Baubo's Garden offers a complete selection of fine lingerie, bras, sleepwear, and more. Known for completely personalized service and expert bra fitting, this comfy boutique focuses on women exploring their inner goddesses. This is a space for women to discover, or rediscover, a sense of beauty and sexiness. Just west of Chicago, Baubo's Garden is also famous for its fun-filled party events.

Debbie Feiler

Q and A

What are your most popular products or services?
Our outstanding collection of baby gifts
and Christening apparel, as well as our
exclusive nursery design service.

People may be surprised to know...
Between my sisters, my daughter, and myself (we
all work here) we have 20 children, ages 2-27!

What or who inspired you to start your business?
My mom, who wanted her daughters to have their
own business, and my dad who believed in our dream.

**What business mistake have you
made that you will not repeat?**
Freaking out when an employee suddenly
quits. There is always a way to get
through it and find a replacement.

What is your indulgence?
A Pontoon boat ride with my husband and family,
while enjoying an appetizer and a martini.

BEAUTIFUL BEGINNINGS

1840 N Clybourn Ave, Chicago, 312.944.1212
shopbeautifulbeginnings.com

Classic. Clean. Sweet.
Beautiful Beginnings is an upscale, full-service baby boutique offering everything you need for your new little one. With layette and Christening departments known throughout the city of Chicago, Beautiful Beginnings will help you decorate your nursery—from simple to elegant.

BEAUTY ON CALL

Chicago, 312.335.5350
beautyoncall.com

GLOSSED & FOUND

Chicago, 312.335.5350
glossedandfound.com

Dependable. Professional. Knowledgeable.
Beauty on Call provides quality beauty and spa services on location for bridal, corporate, and retail events.
Glossed & Found is an online magazine featuring the best in beauty, fashion, and lifestyle in Chicago.

Q and A

What are your most popular products or services?
Beauty on Call: hair, makeup, and manicures on location for weddings and special occasions. Glossed & Found: videos featuring top designers.

People may be surprised to know...
Although I am considered a beauty expert in the industry, I am the worst makeup artist! I am great at finding and managing top artists, and have extensive product knowledge, but you don't want me doing your makeup!

What or who inspired you to start your business?
I was previously a cosmetic buyer for Nordstrom and saw a void in the industry, so I started the first staffing agency in the country focused on beauty.

How do you spend your free time?
Traveling with my husband and spending quality time with my 1-year-old twins and 2-year-old daughter.

Where is your favorite place to go with your girlfriends?
Anywhere where there is sun, sand, and margaritas!

Stacey Roney

BEDROOMS BY BRYNNE

773.960.8619
bedroomsbybrynne.com

Inviting. Sensual. Bold.
Bedrooms by Brynne offers a wide array of services, ranging from the simple—like helping you select just the right custom bedding—to a complete and elaborate renovation of your bedroom. Brynne will design your bedroom interior for restful sleep, repose and a place to be playful. Whatever you have a taste for, Bedrooms by Brynne imagines and fuses the very best version of who you are… into your bedroom.

Brynne Rinderknecht

Q and A

What are your most popular products or services?
Interior design for the home—specializing in the bedroom, and event design for weddings and special occasions.

People may be surprised to know...
I worked as a set designer and stylist for *Playboy* for more than nine years.

What or who inspired you to start your business?
Seeing the movie *The Pillowbook* inspired me to study interior design, and a long road trip alone motivated me to start my own business.

Who is your role model or mentor?
Andree Putman, Zaha Hadid, and Katherine Hepburn.

How do you spend your free time?
Practicing yoga, snowboarding, traveling, listening to music, watching films, and visiting with good friends for mad laughs.

What is your indulgence?
Fresh-cut flowers, mohair, fine linens, and art.

BELLYBUM BOUTIQUE

4347 N Lincoln Ave, Chicago, 773.868.0944
bellybumboutique.com, Twitter: @BellybumMom

Green. Stylish. Nurturing.
Bellybum Boutique is one of the newest and freshest additions to Chicago's "green baby scene."
A unique celebration of mamma bellies and baby butts, Bellybum carries designer maternal-transition and nursing wear—cloth diapers, organic children's wear, baby gear, gifts, and accessories. More importantly, it is a support center dedicated to providing families with healthy lifestyle options, as well as expert prenatal, postnatal, and parenting education and resources.

Ellen Sternweiler

Q and A

What are your most popular products or services?
Designer women's transition, nursing, and children's wear; cloth diapers, eco-friendly baby gear and accessories; parenting resources, support, and classes.

What or who inspired you to start your business?
The joys, complications, and trials of pregnancy and parenthood compelled me to create a one-of-a-kind community of support for parents.

Who is your role model or mentor?
My friend, Nina, who showed me being a mother and a strong businesswoman, and following my heart were all possible.

How do you spend your free time?
When I'm not with my husband and three young children—I'm happiest camping, kayaking, or fly fishing in the wilderness.

What is your indulgence?
Going to a spa and treating myself to a massage.

Michelle Garcia

Q and A

What are your most popular products or services?
The Take A Hike scone is most popular, as well as our S'mores brownie, cupcakes, and amazing 3d cakes.

People may be surprised to know...
We pride ourselves on our integrity. Anyone who doubts us is welcome to peek into production and see exactly what we are all about.

How do you spend your free time?
I spend my free time with my children and my husband. I choose not to make plans without them. Every second counts.

What is your indulgence?
Bacon. I just love it. I was vegan for a good portion of my life and I craved it the whole time.

Where is your favorite place to go with your girlfriends?
We love to go to craft fairs, such as Renegade, and to neighborhood festivals.

THE BLEEDING HEART BAKERY

1955 W Belmont Ave, Chicago, 773.327.6934
thebleedingheartbakery.com, Twitter: @bleeding_heart

SMASH CAKE

2961 N Lincoln Ave, Chicago, 773.281.2353
smashcakechicago.com, Twitter: @smashchicago

Organic. Sustainable. Punk Rock.

The Bleeding Heart Bakery is dedicated to creating delicious and inventive pastries, cakes, and breads, using all organic and locally produced products. After six years and multiple awards—including "Chicago's Best Bakery" three years running, six *Food Network* challenges, and Michelle's win as ACF pastry chef of the year—The Bleeding Heart Bakery has won a coveted spot among Chicago's top pastry destinations. Smash Cake came later out of a love for children and a desire to offer a place for kids to enjoy organic goodies. Smash Cake is open during the week for drop-ins and on the weekends for birthday parties.

BRAMBLE

115 N Oak Park Ave, Oak Park, 708.386.6800
bramble.biz

Gift. Home. Garden.
Bramble features an ever-changing assortment of eclectic gifts and home goods inspired by the beauty of nature. Set in a gorgeous historic building in the heart of Oak Park, Bramble's expansive space enables a shopping experience that is pleasant, inspiring, and sure to impress even the most discerning seekers of retail therapy. Come enjoy the blissful discovery of beautiful things at Bramble.

Q and A

What are your most popular products or services?
Bee Glow lanterns, Napa soap products, handmade leaf tiles, French table linens, and Japanese ceramics.

People may be surprised to know...
We have a great collection of jewelry, scarves, and other wearable items.

What or who inspired you to start your business?
The realization that there were others like me who had to travel far and wide to find interesting things, yet held a strong appreciation for the value of shopping local.

Who is your role model or mentor?
Family and friends, but most of all, my dog Schroeder and all he stands for: inquisitive nature, cheerful demeanor, and love for all living things. In other words, "wag more, bark less."

How do you spend your free time?
Strolling around this lovely town, sitting on the porch with a book, or packing my bags and getting on the road.

Danah Fisher

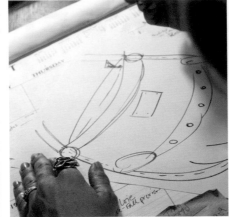

Brynn Capella

 Q and A

People may be surprised to know...
I don't have a fashion degree. I am a
journalism graduate and worked in radio
and records for about eight years.

What or who inspired you to start your business?
My mom always taught me I could do
whatever I set my mind to, my sister dared
me and my friends supported me.

What business mistake have you
made that you will not repeat?
Over-designing and producing of a season. I
learned to keep it small, simple and clean.

How do you spend your free time?
With family (especially my nieces Samantha and
Sophie, and my nephew, Dylan) and friends in
Chicago, San Diego, Los Angeles, and Honolulu.

What is your indulgence?
Besides handbags? Shoes! Accessories. I love
local jewelry designers, too. I can't forget
denim—I wear it almost everyday.

BRYNN CAPELLA

Chicago, 323.559.5299
brynncapella.com, Twitter: @brynncapella

Fresh. Functional. Timeless.
Brynn Capella has found the perfect mix of her laid-back Southern California upbringing and her new urban Chicago lifestyle. Ultimately, however, it is her attention to every detail (classic styles, affordable prices, great hardware and distinctive textiles and leathers) that sets her apart from the often over-styled and over-priced department store lines. No mass-production either, as she still has her entire limited edition collection handcrafted in Chicago!

What is your indulgence?

" *I absolutely love Vosges Chocolates. They are my favorite indulgence* **"**

Agnes B. Miles, Love, Lulu Mae

Julia Buckingham Edelmann

Q and A

What are your most popular products or services?
Creating homes with a unique twist on tradition.
Offering all facets of interior design services.

People may be surprised to know...
That designing your home or office should be fun!

What or who inspired you to start your business?
I was inspired by the look on the face of my first
design client... total happiness and excitement!

What business mistake have you
made that you will not repeat?
Lacking the confidence to say what I really believed.

How do you spend your free time?
Posting on my blog, materialgirlsblog.com,
reading other design blogs and devouring
all design magazines for inspiration.

What is your indulgence?
Taking the day off to explore new shops and
neighborhoods for the perfect artifacts for my clients.

BUCKINGHAM INTERIORS + DESIGN

301 Sheridan Road, Wilmette, 312.933.8359
buckinghamID.com

Sophisticated. Imaginative. Enthusiastic.
Julia Buckingham Edelmann is the founder and owner of Buckingham ID, a Chicago-based interiors firm specializing in residential and commercial design. Julia's fascination with interior design and her passion for antiques stem from studying merchandising and marketing at the University of Arizona and owning both a Cincinnati-based antiques store and a Chicago art and design showroom. Julia travels around the world to provide her clients with intriguing one-of-a-kind artifacts.

Kari Vanick

Q and A

What are your most popular products or services?
Doggy daycare, overnight boarding, and grooming.

People may be surprised to know...
We have webcams on all the play areas so you can check up on your dog online at any time!

What or who inspired you to start your business?
Jacquie Pierson, my best friend from San Diego. A marvelous woman who owns a dog grooming business *and* a restaurant.

How do you spend your free time?
I love sports—snowboarding, wakeboarding, quadding, scuba diving, hiking, white-water rafting, rock climbing—you name it, I'm there.

Where is your favorite place to go with your girlfriends?
Hiking in the park with the girls and the dogs. Girls Rock. Dogs Rule.

CAMP BOW WOW MCHENRY

3107 W IL Route 120, McHenry, 815.385.PAWS (7297)
campbowwow.com/mchenry, Twitter: @CBWMcHenry

Safe. Clean. Fun.

Camp Bow Wow McHenry is Chicago's northwest suburbs' premier doggy day and overnight camp. They provide the ultimate experience where your dog can be a dog in a safe, clean, and fun environment. Webcams are available on all play areas to watch your furry friend online anytime. And at Camp Bow Wow, hugs, butt scratches, and belly rubs are all free!

CANDYALITY

3425 N Southport Ave, Chicago, 773.472.7800
The Shops at North Bridge, 520 N Michigan Ave, Chicago
candyality.com, Twitter: @candyalitygirl

Unique. Exciting. One-of-a-Kind.
Derived from the concept of associating candy with your personality profile, Candyality offers carefully selected, highly indulgent, quirky, nostalgic, and unique sweets that have both lasting and universal appeal. At the heart of Candyality's customer service philosophy is the desire to uncover a universal connection through confections.

Q and A

People may be surprised to know...
You really are what you eat! Candy does not lie.

What or who inspired you to start your business?
As a former sales and training executive, I used candy profiling techniques to determine selling personalities. With spikes in sales productivity, I watched people connect with their "inner candy eater!"

Who is your role model or mentor?
Willy Wonka, of course! He uses pure imagination, mixes everything with love, and makes the world taste good!

What business mistake have you made that you will not repeat?
Not hiring enough people, and trying to do it all myself.

How do you spend your free time?
At my beach house with my family.

Where is your favorite place to go with your girlfriends?
I'll go anywhere with my girlfriends—shopping, mani-pedi's, Nomi Gardens, Sepia on Jefferson, the patio at Newport Bar & Grill, Southport Lanes...

Terese McDonald

CHICAGO KIDS BOOKSTORE AND MORE

3453 N Southport, Chicago, 773.47.BOOKS
chicagokidsbooks.com

Lively. Warm. Fun.
From their comfortable, playful atmosphere, to their huge selection of books, Chicago Kids Bookstore is the perfect place to dive into reading! In addition to providing Chicago's Southport neighborhood with an amazing selection of children's and young adult literature, they also carry gifts, interactive games, and puzzles for children of all ages. Dedicated to building a strong literary foundation for Chicago's youth, Chicago Kids Bookstore donates a portion of their earnings to various child advocacy groups.

Nina Gardner, manager and director of marketing and PR (Owner Kara Thompson is not pictured)

Q and A

People may be surprised to know...
How strongly we feel about supporting local people and local authors! Chicago authors have great stories to tell, and we want to share them with as many people as possible! Chicago Kids Bookstore hosts several authors each month for refreshments, readings, and signings.

What or who inspired you to start your business?
The statistic that stuck in our head was that a big indicator of failure as an adult was the inability to read well by the third grade. That impacted us so much that we knew we had to do something. We wanted to have books that appealed to all ages, in places that were comfortable to spend time in. We wanted to reach out to the community and do our part to promote literacy, so that statistic didn't come true.

Who is your role model or mentor?
Corporations that have been successful in selling a product, raising awareness about the product, and promoting the best use of product, all while being active, positive members of their communities.

53

Norma Alanis

 Q and A

What are your most popular products or services?
Our most popular services are Chocoholic manicure, pedicure, facial and massage. The soak, scrub, lotion, and masque is made with organic Peruvian chocolate. It's simply decadent!

Who is your role model or mentor?
My mother. She has an incredible work ethic, is very resilient, and has a super can-do positive attitude.

How do you spend your free time?
What free time? In addition to being actively involved with my son's extracurricular activities, I founded Pilsen's first farmer's market. It gives me great satisfaction to do something for the community.

What is your indulgence?
I am a chocolate and shoe junkie.

Where is your favorite place to go with your girlfriends?
Concerts at Millennium Park.

CHOCOLATE FOR YOUR BODY SPA

1743 S Halsted St, Chicago, 312.226.0777
chocolateforyourbody.com

Friendly. Urban. Chocolatey.
Opened in 2007, this hidden gem located in Pilsen's Art District offers a chocolate-centric
menu of rejuvenating spa treatments. Our goal is to pamper our guests with the most
natural products available while maintaining affordability. CFYB Spa offers unique beauty
treatments to satisfy every sweet tooth... Because every*body* deserves a little chocolate!

SINFUL

Mary Winslow

Q and A

What are your most popular products or services?
The 20-piece cookie assortment is our most popular product, though the "show them you care" bundle is also up there.

People may be surprised to know...
When I was young, I wanted to be a fashion designer.

Who is your role model or mentor?
That's easy: my mom.

What business mistake have you made that you will not repeat?
Staying on a career path—publishing sales— that didn't really make me happy.

How do you spend your free time?
When I'm not in the kitchen—and even when I am!—I love spending time with my family. I also enjoy riding bikes, watching movies, and going out to eat.

What is your indulgence?
A good glass (or two) of wine.

CHOCOLATE GOURMET & TAKE THE CAKE

312.850.1051
chocolategourmet.com, takethecakeetc.com, Twitter: @chocogourmet

Down-to-earth. Avant-garde. Visionary.

Mary Winslow gained her reputation as one of Chicago's premier wedding cake designers at Take the Cake, the bakeshop she founded in the 1990s. Mary's creative impulses later led her to sweets of a simpler nature, and Chocolate Gourmet was born. Through Chocolate Gourmet, Mary and her team make irresistible treats, including Damn Good Cookies, Ugly Truffles, and rugelach.

COLETTE

312.320.4665
coletteltd.com

Stylish. Exquisite. Inspired.
Colette is Chicago's favorite eco-chic home fragrance company. Handmade and hand-packaged with care, it's that personal touch that has made Colette's creations such treasured gifts. Each item comes in its own hat box container, making it a luxurious indulgence. Colette candles and amazing fragrance products can be found in Chicago's finest boutiques.

Colette Gleeson

Q and A

What are your most popular products or services?
The Modern Collection candles—French Fig and Twig.

People may be surprised to know...
I design all of our packaging and fragrances, so my life finds its way into everything we produce. Everything I encounter translates to my company or to a new product.

What or who inspired you to start your business?
My mother. Our home was always tastefully decorated with a blend of contemporary and traditional designs that beautifully conveyed my mom's unique style. Even when she was not expecting company, candles were always burning. I developed my design style by combining the influences of old and new to create something beautiful.

What business mistake have you made that you will not repeat?
Not listening to what my customers say. It may not be easy to hear all of the feedback and comments, but it's priceless information.

59

Q and A

Colette Green

People may be surprised to know...
All our staff members are required and committed to on-going education. We also do the best hair extensions in town!

What or who inspired you to start your business?
The creative outlet from styling hair, the client interaction, and the overall style and vibrance of the salon business attracted me most.

Who is your role model or mentor?
People who have a dream and dare to make it come true.

How do you spend your free time?
I enjoy time at home with my family, dinner out with friends, live music, cooking, gardening, bike riding ... too many to list!

Where is your favorite place to go with your girlfriends?
My girlfriends and I enjoy going to Topo Gigio on Wells Street for dinner, and we often go out to see a concert.

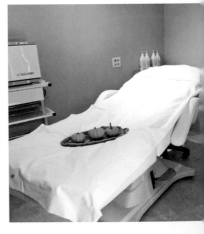

COLETTE SALON AND SPA

100 E Walton Level 3, Chicago, 312.944.1409
colettesalonspa.com

Stylish. Flirty. Vibrant,
Colette Salon and Spa, located just steps off Michigan Ave in the Gold Coast, features a top-notch team of stylists and spa specialists. Hair care services include cuts, colors, Brazilian straighteners, and expert hair extensions, while Colette's experienced spa staff provide nail care, waxing, facials, and much more. Voted one of Chicago's Top Salons by *Chicago Magazine*, Colette Salon and Spa is an urban oasis for salon and spa services.

COLORI ECO PAINT BOUTIQUE

2243 W North Ave, Chicago, 773.252.4923
colorichicago.com, Twitter: @ColoriEcoPaint, facebook.com/ColoriEcoPaint

Hip. Green. Fun.
Colori is a one-of-a-kind, eco-friendly paint boutique that caters to your individuality, as
well as your desire to be environmentally conscious. With local Chicago roots and a mission
to connect with local businesses and consumers that share the same eco-frienly values,
Colori is passionate, independent, earth-conscious, true-color, enlightening, and fun!

Q and A

What are your most popular products or services?
In-home and in-store color consultations,
and environmentally-friendly paint.

People may be surprised to know...
I used to be in the road construction business.

What or who inspired you to start your business?
I wanted to redefine the way people experience
color when shopping for environmentally-friendly
paint. By offering color consulting in the form
of color therapy, we take into consideration the
unique needs of each client, while, at the same
time, educating them about the impact our choices
have on our environment and our health.

Who is your role model or mentor?
My parents, who came to the United States from Italy.

How do you spend your free time?
Going to see live music, cooking, and
hanging out with friends and family.

Michelle Quaranta

Tami
Conway

 Q and A

What are your most popular products or services?
Our exercise classes! We have great retail products, but it is our classes that bring people into the studio.

People may be surprised to know...
That this workout is for everyone! We offer an amazing workout for all different ability levels, sexes, shapes, and sizes—and the best part is everyone sees the results.

What or who inspired you to start your business?
My husband. Without his help, support, and love, I wouldn't be where I am today.

How do you spend your free time?
Quality family time with my husband, Brett, daughter Quinn, and our dog Baxter. Family walks are my favorite!

What is your indulgence?
Wine. I love having a glass of wine at dinner with my husband, catching up with girlfriends at someone's house, or for no reason at all.

THE DAILEY METHOD CHICAGO

1714 N Damen Ave, Ste 2N, Chicago, 773.904.8913
thedaileymethod.com

Effective. Addictive. Empowering.
The Dailey Method is a unique combination of ballet barre work, core conditioning, stretching, and orthopedic exercises. This challenging one-hour class effectively strengthens, tones, and lengthens the entire body. Light weights are utilized to define the upper body, while mat and ballet barre work target the thighs, seat, and abdominals. Each muscle group is worked through high repetition using a small range of motion, then alternately stretched to lengthen the muscles.

Darcy McGrath

 Q and A

What or who inspired you to start your business?
My Mother. She was a very inspiring entrepreneur with charm, vision, and an endless sense of passion, humor, and fashion!

People may be surprised to know...
I bicycled through the Southern French Alps, and I am huge animal lover.

Who is your role model or mentor?
I have been very honored to know and work with legendary talents, photographers, and directors. However my first insights to business and travel I owe to my family and best friends.

What is your indulgence?
Beautiful candles, vintage linens, and sea shell collecting.

Where is your favorite place to go with your girlfriends?
Dinner... anywhere!

As seen in InStyle Weddings. Mary Henebry

DARCY MCGRATH BEAUTY

Chicago, 312.337.1353
darcymcgrathbeauty.com

Private. Empowering. Beautifying.

As a celebrity makeup artist and product guru nearly all her life, Darcy McGrath makes practical magic of it all. With more than 20 years in the business, she is known as one of the most well-respected studio makeup artist in the industry. Darcy's defining services are Mastering Your Makeup™ and Beauty and the Bride™, and she was making house calls before it was hip!

Lynda Wood

Q and A

What or who inspired you to start your business?
My love and appreciation for beautiful fashion, and my desire to protect, restore, and preserve it for future generations.

Who is your role model or mentor?
I am grateful to my parents for their courage, extraordinary work ethic, passion for excellence, and love and devotion to their family and craft.

What business mistake have you made that you will not repeat?
Mistakes are essential to professional growth. They can and have been life's greatest teachers.

How do you spend your free time?
My work is my passion so it occupies a great deal of my time. However, spending free time with my family is what truly fills me up.

What is your indulgence?
Just ask my husband, Rick! David Yurman and John Hardy jewelry, and Chanel handbags!

DAVIS IMPERIAL CLEANERS

3325 W Bryn Mawr Ave, Chicago, 773.267.4560
davisimperial.com

Professional. Experienced. Uncompromising.
Davis Imperial Cleaners, a certified couture cleaner™, is recognized as one of the top 10 fabricare specialists in the world by Leading Cleaners Internationale, as well as "best couture cleaner" by *Chicago Magazine*. Established in 1956, Davis Imperial Cleaners is the first drycleaner in Illinois certified as a "green cleaner" by the Green Cleaners Council. Providing pick-up and delivery and FabricareByMail™, Davis is proud to be referred by Chicago's premier bridal salons, specialty boutiques, couture designers, event planners, and hotels.

THE DENIM LOUNGE

43 E Oak St, Chicago, 312.642.6403
2004 W Roscoe St, 773.935.2820
thedenimlounge.com, Twitter: @thedenimlounge

MADISON AND FRIENDS

43 E Oak St, Chicago, 312.642.6403
madisonandfriends.com

Stylish. Quality. Contemporary.
The Denim Lounge has been offering the best in denim for more than seven years, and has more than 20 of the hottest, newest denim lines. Madison and Friends has been an Oak Street institution for 13 years. The boutique carries the most unique clothes, shoes, and accessories for kids—from newborn through size 14.

Wendi Gordon Shelist

Q and A

People may be surprised to know...
The Oak St. location has a "butt cam" so you can see how the denim shapes your rear on a plasma TV!

What or who inspired you to start your business?
My daughter, Madison. My husband and I opened our first store when she was 6 months old.

Who is your role model or mentor?
My father, who has owned Bravco on Oak Street for 30 years.

What business mistake have you made that you will not repeat?
Opening new stores in bad locations just because the landlord promised the moon.

How do you spend your free time?
I like to work out and spend time with my husband, kids, and dogs. I love living in the city and walking on the Lakefront.

What is your indulgence?
Shoes and chocolate!

71

DILLY LILY

742 W Fullerton Pkwy, Chicago, 773.404.0602
dillylily.com, twitter: @thedillylily

Delightful. Delicious. De-lovely.
Inspired by fashion, travel, and nature, Christine Noelle and the talented staff at Dilly Lily
create signature floral pieces for their loyal clientele. Colorful, trendy, or classic, each design
is an individual expression, a work of art. From your everyday wishes to your wedding day
dreams, Dilly Lily translates your style into flowers. Just stop by and see for yourself!

Christine Noelle

Q and A

What are your most popular products or services?
Flowers, flowers, flowers, flowers, flowers!

People may be surprised to know...
I thought I was going to be a fashion designer.

Who or what inspired you to start your business?
I come from a long line of entrepreneurs.

Who is your role model or mentor?
My mother has always inspired me
to push myself creatively.

What business mistake have you made
that you will not repeat?
I am a perfectionist, so it pains me to make the
smallest mistake. I certainly can't make it twice!

What is your indulgence?
Champagne with dinner at Blackbird.

Where is your favorite place to go with your girlfriends?
I will go anywhere with my girlfriends. We love to travel.

DOLLYBIRD JEWELRY

Chicago, 773.636.7140
dollybirddesign.com

Rustic. Simple. Modern.
Metalsmith and designer Katie Johansson creates individually handcrafted pieces for Dollybird Jewelry, based on one-of-a-kind designs. Inventing her own trends, she gets her inspiration from any boulder, crag, crystal, gem, grain, gravel, jewel, metal, mineral, ore, pebble, or rock. Her mission is to create jewelry that is original in form and timeless in style, so that it can be passed on with ages to come.

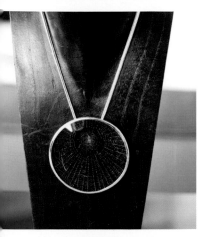

Katie Johansson

Q and A

What are your most popular products or services?
The Dollybird Arachnid Collection—real cobwebs preserved in glass. The copper dome ring, making metal represent a stone. All hallmarked, one-of-a-kind stones.

People may be surprised to know...
The term "dollybird" is rather old-fashioned. It was used mainly in the 1960s to mean a fashionable young girl.

What business mistake have you made that you will not repeat?
Turning my back on my gut. Always believe what your heart tells you first.

Who or what inspired you to start your business?
Jewelry is becoming just another mass-produced product. I was frustrated with overseas production of high-volume, inexpensive finished goods. In the Victorian Era, jewelry was made to pass on. I wanted to bring some of that back. Jewelry should represent something unique and special for the buyer—a one-of-a-kind talisman, a sweet memory, or a sentimental token to hold on to and to pass on.

75

ELIZABETH GRACE

2438 N Clark St, Chicago, 773.477.9830
elizabethgrace.com

Charming. Creative. Classic.
Located in a vintage walk-up in Lincoln Park, Elizabeth Grace is Chicago's premier paperie
and gift store, offering high-end stationery lines (Sugar Paper, Crane & Co., Kate Spade),
exclusive wedding invitation collections (Ceci New York, Elum, Vera Wang), and an assortment
of gifts for the discriminating shopper. Known for her impeccable taste and design savvy,
owner Laura Manteuffel offers personalized service unparalleled in Chicago.

DINE, DANCE, CELEBRATE
AT HALF AFTER SIX O'CLOCK
THE IVY ROOM AT TREE STUDIOS
TWELVE EAST OHIO STREET
CHICAGO
black tie invited

Laura
Manteuffel

Q and A

What are your most popular products or services?
Our own custom-designed stationery and invitations!

What or who inspired you to start your business?
One of my corporate clients asked me to design her wedding invitations. After the invitations were in the mail, we put together all the coordinating little extras for her wedding, and I was hooked. One thing led to another and, here we are many years later in a great shop with more than 30 beautiful lines of stationery.

Who is your role model or mentor?
I have been so lucky to learn from so many talented people, both in the design community and the wedding business, but my dad is the best role model and mentor anyone could ever have.

How do you spend your free time?
I wish I could spend all my free time diving in deep blue water from a boat in the South Pacific.

ELLIE D PERFUME

elliedperfume.com

Elegant. Youthful. Classic.

Jessica Dunne founded Ellie D Perfume to create scents inspired by childhood memories of her elegant grandmother, perfume aficionado Eleanor "Ellie" Dunne. Jessica is dedicated to creating luxurious products rooted in the time-honored art of perfumery. She worked one-on-one with master French perfumer Michel Roudnitska to create the fragrances. Everything is created in small batches to maintain quality and authenticity.

Jessica Dunne

Q and A

What are your most popular products or services?
Both scents, Ellie and Ellie Nuit, have a loyal following. It's impossible to pick favorites!

People may be surprised to know...
It took about two years of trips to France and hundreds of samples sent across the ocean to create the fragrances.

What or who inspired you to start your business?
My grandmother and my mother were my biggest inspirations. I have vivid memories of watching them dab on their perfume before an evening out, and I wanted to try to capture their elegance with a modern, youthful spin.

How do you spend your free time?
With my husband, Brian, and my daughter Laine, cooking, traveling, and visiting friends.

What is your indulgence?
Other than traveling, most of my indulgences involve food! I love wine, cheese, and trying new restaurants.

Barb Skupien

Q and A

What are your most popular products or services?
Unique, independently made jewelry.

People may be surprised to know...
Before opening Embellish Boutique,
I had no retail experience.

What or who inspired you to start your business?
A year-long trip around the world taught me that
I could do anything I dreamed, so I finally did.

Who is your role model or mentor?
My youngest sister.

What business mistake have you
made that you will not repeat?
Trusting that color swatches online
represent the color I'll receive!

How do you spend your free time?
I don't have much free time, but
when I do, I love to read.

EMBELLISH BOUTIQUE

4161 N Lincoln Ave, Chicago, 773.525.4400
embellishchicago.com

Unique. Independent. Beautiful.
Embellish Boutique is an accessories boutique that features jewelry and handbags by independent artists and designers, many of whom are local. If Embellish Boutique carries it, it's unique and it's affordable!

ENGAGING EVENTS BY ALI, INC

Chicago, 773.777.2299
engagingeventsbyali.com, Twitter: @AliPhillips

Personable. Organized. Creative.
Ali Phillips of Engaging Events by Ali, Inc—one of Chicago's top wedding consultants—delivers a magical and fun wedding experience to her brides and grooms. Her organization skills, negotiation savvy, and appreciation for the "art" of customer service have been invaluable in working with vendors, staying within a budget, and creating beautiful, flawless events for her clients.

Q and A

What are your most popular products or services?
Most clients book our full wedding planning services. I am with the client throughout their entire engagement, to assure that they are on schedule for a perfect and unique wedding day.

People may be surprised to know...
I am a very good cook. I love coming home from a long day masterminding a wonderful meal.

How do you spend your free time?
I love to spend time on the lake with my husband and our dog. When it is not wedding season in Chicago, we love to travel in the United States and beyond. I am always researching our next big adventure.

Where is your favorite place to go with your girlfriends?
Any spa is good for time with girlfriends. There is nothing better than a day with your friends, unwinding, getting spa treatments, and going out for a nice dinner afterwards.

Ali Phillips

What business mistake have you made that you will not repeat?

"Not taking risks. Reinventing yourself and your business is a must. Don't doubt your ideas, even when they don't work out"

Michelle and Melissa Gomez,
M.GO Fashion Salon

ESSENTIAL BLUEPRINTS

Chicago, 312.224.8977
essentialblueprints.com

Unique. Inviting. Memorable.
Essential Blueprints (EB) captures the soul of a woman's pregnancy by creating a vehicle for documenting her experiences. The EB experience supports the mother in being introspective with her own words. Professional photography sessions capture the beauty of her journey. Essential Blueprints ensures that each woman comes away with a personalized photo journal along with a deeper spiritual and emotional connection with her newborn and herself.

Claude-Aline
Nazaire

What are your most popular products or services?
Our most popular product is the "Any Day Now" package. It begins blueprinting a client's pregnancy during their last trimester.

Who is your role model or mentor?
I am blessed to have many role models and mentors in my life that encourage, me to pursue my business. It begins at home with my parents, sisters and several amazing girlfriends. My photography mentor is Ollie Dantzler.

What business mistake have you made that you will not repeat?
Not delegating responsibility and using resources available to me. Never be afraid to ask for advice.

Where is your favorite place to go with your girlfriends?
My girlfriends and I love The Matchbox. It's a very well-known Chicago bar with the most amazing owner and bar staff. The drinks are amazing and it's the perfect spot to unwind after a hectic day.

87

Q and A

Annette E. Sollars

What or who inspired you to start your business?
A bland world sorely in need of more color.

Who is your role model or mentor?
Martha Stewart. She fought her way to the top
in what is sadly still a man's business world.

**What business mistake have you
made that you will not repeat?**
Buying into the misguided notion that optometry
services were necessary to my opticianry practice.

How do you spend your free time?
When you are self-employed, you
don't have much free time!

What is your indulgence?
Quadruple decaf lattes and home-cooked dinners
almost every night, made by my devoted husband.

**Where is your favorite place to
go with your girlfriends?**
Out shopping to other independent,
locally-owned businesses.

EYE WANT

1543 N Milwaukee Ave, Chicago, 773.782.1744
eyewanteyewear.com

Incomparable. Unconstrained. Uninhibited.
Eye Want has been setting the standard for face fashion since 1997, carrying an unparalleled selection of distinctive frames, and spawning numerous imitators. They carry only fine eyewear of American, European, and Japanese manufacture. Owner Annette E. Sollars believes her customers deserve the best, and she will never compromise in delivering it to them.

FIVE ACCESSORIES

Andersonville Galleria, 5247 N Clark St, 773.878.8570
fiveaccessories.com, Twitter: @fiveACCESSORIES

Eco-friendly. Sustainable. Socially Conscious.
five ACCESSORIES is a socially conscious company offering eco-friendly and fair-trade
handbags and accessories. Their products come from five countries. For each handbag sale,
five ACCESSORIES donates $5 to a worthy charity in the locale where it was handmade.
Their mission is to create income-generating programs, to donate a large portion of
sales to worthy charities, and to foster the use of sustainable material in fashion.

Christine Hutchison

Q and A

What are your most popular products or services?
Our eco-friendly bamboo, wicker, and coconut shell handbags from our Bali Collection.

People may be surprised to know...
We have launched a new income-generating program, called Off The Street, that offers handmade accessories, such as recycled picture frames and bottle top barrettes, all handmade by the vendors of Chicago's StreetWise.

What or who inspired you to start your business?
In particular, a Balinese tour guide we met while traveling to Bali, Indonesia. He spoke of how an American couple changed his life many years ago by their act of kindness. We wanted to be that next American couple to touch the lives of others in developing nations.

Where is your favorite place to go with your girlfriends?
Overlooking the Chicago lakefront (hopefully on a sailboat) on a nice summer day).

Julia Nash

Q and A

What are your most popular products or services?
Design oriented goodies. Alessi housewares, Ugly Dolls, and candles by Skeem are a few of our top sellers.

People may be surprised to know...
Fly Bird does not rent tuxedos, sell birds, or do pedicures. These are all pretty frequent questions, believe it or not!

What or who inspired you to start your business?
The need for a store in Oak Park showcasing subcultures, DIY, and modern design.

How do you spend your free time?
Reading, running, and cooking for my family.

What is your indulgence?
Buying something super amazing for the shop just because I love it, even when I'm not so sure it will sell.

Where is your favorite place to go with your girlfriends?
My backyard with some good wine and great food.

FLY BIRD

719 Lake St, Oak Park, 708.383.3330
fly-bird.net

In Good Fun.
Fly Bird is a specialty gift shop deeply rooted in the Oak Park community, chock full of curiosities for the happy home, body, and mind. We are here to share our love and excitement for new design, as well as products with great style and humor. The truth is... we sell only what we love.

FREDDA ID

Chicago, 773.227.6701
FreddaID.com, Twitter: @TheFreddaID

Authentic. Empowering. Visionary.
Fredda has moved image consulting into a new field of personal identity, combining it with business identity, as a vehicle for personal growth. She offers personal, business, and life style coaching, lectures, seminars, and retreats. All can empower you, your business, or organization. She will help you create an image and life style of personal power and authenticity. Based in Chicago, available everywhere.

Q and A

What are your most popular products or services?
The Energy of Style™ coaching sessions; The
Challenge of Authenticity™ lecture or keynote;
In Your Own Image™ seminars and retreats.

People may be surprised to know...
I am the only life coach, speaker, and trainer
that uses personal image as a vehicle for self-
actualization and spiritual growth.

What or who inspired you to start your business?
When working with the world's most beautiful
models, I found they had the same issues
of self-concept as ordinary women.

Who is your role model or mentor?
My lawyer father taught me the art of the deal. My
mother—artist, stylist, sculptor—is the diva of lifestyle.

What business mistake have you made
that you will not repeat?
Thomas Edison had 3,000 failed prototypes
for the light bulb. Every choice is an
opportunity to move towards your goals.

Fredda

G BOUTIQUE

2131 N Damen, Chicago, 773.235.1234
1451 W Fullerton, Chicago
boutiqueg.com, Twitter: @gboutique

Feminine. Sexy. Discrete.
G Boutique is Chicago's spiciest lingerie and toy store. G is for women and men who love women. The boutique offers exquisite lingerie from across the globe, a great staff to help you choose just the right toy, and the perfect options for "girl's night out" parties.

Cheryl Sloane, Debra Phillips, and Kari Kupcinet-Kriser

Q and A

What are your most popular products or services?
Pin-up workshops, sex ed, Hanky Panky, Cosabella, the we-vibe.

People may be surprised to know...
How important a good lubricant is.

Who is your role model or mentor?
Our moms and Sue Holleb from Certain Something.

What business mistake have you made that you will not repeat?
Ordering too much lingerie just because it was so beautiful.

How do you spend your free time?
Playing.

Where is your favorite place to go with your girlfriends?
The Beach.

Q and A

Lauren Cavallo Runzel

What are your most popular products or services?
Tops, jeans, dresses, accessories, and jewelry from great designers, such as Gryphon, Pencey, and Elizabeth & James.

What or who inspired you to start your business?
I am a cancer survivor and decided to follow a dream I'd had for years since I learned that life is short.

Who is your role model or mentor?
Brana Wolf, Carlyne Cerf du Dudzelle and Franca Sozzani are stylists that I worked with in Europe and influenced me big time!

How do you spend your free time?
With my six children.

What is your indulgence?
Shoes, shoes, shoes!

Where is your favorite place to go with your girlfriends?
Either Union or Bluestone in Evanston, or the garden at Topogigio in the City.

GAVIN EVANSTON

1939 Central St, Evanston, 847.328.7407
shopgavin.com

Chic. Liberating. Rule-breaking.
We believe *CS Magazine* said it best in their June 2009 issue: "From Paris catwalks to
Evanston sidewalks—that's the idea behind women's boutique GAVIN. Ex-model-
turned-mother-of-six Lauren Cavallo Runzel knows a thing or two about effortless
style from her days walking the runways, and now she is passing her wisdom."

GENACELLI SALON

2829 N Sheffield Ave, Chicago, 773.248.8822
genacelli.com, Twitter: @GenacelliSalon

Savvy. Modern. Relaxed.
Find your look at Lake View/Lincoln Park's cutting-edge upscale hair and skin-care salon. Combining modern methods with luxury hair care, Genacelli Salon's award-winning team creates original hair styles just right for an urban lifestyle, and just right for you. Both women and men are welcome to experience the positive vibe the boutique salon offers. The Genacelli team will get personal so you get noticed!

Cynthia Porcelli

What are your most popular products or services?
Kerastase and Shu Uemura retail
products and treatments,

People may be surprised to know...
I am a great cook.

What or who inspired you to start your business?
My exposure to art. It's all creative.

Who is your role model or mentor?
Coco Chanel and Pablo Picasso for their endless passion.

How do you spend your free time?
Free time? With my husband.

What is your indulgence?
Prada, perfume, and shoes.

Where is your favorite place to go with your girlfriends?
RL for lunch and Hollywood Beach to hang.

GLANCER MAGAZINE

Naperville & Wheaton/Glen Ellyn, 630.428.4387
glancermagazine.com, Twitter: @glancermagazine

Creative. Revealing. Adored.
Delivering community living at a glance, Glancer Magazine is an appealing choice for suburban residents with urban taste and style. Glancer's award-winning concept provides local flavor, with each issue providing in-depth coverage of unique, local finds. Monthly features include dining and cabaret, community events, celebrity appearances, fashion and style, culture and the arts, family living, home and garden, charitable events, business features, and community spirit.

Q and A

What or who inspired you to start your business?
My mother, who passed away when I was 20 (she was 44). She was always so smart and creative. We used to brainstorm about fun business ideas. I guess it's in my blood.

Who is your role model or mentor?
I have several, and each represents a different part of my life. Some that come to mind are Tomi (my sister), Renee (my neighbor), and Christine (my best friend). While we are all very different, they balance me.

How do you spend your free time?
At home, with my husband and our 5-year-old daughter. We love carnivals, water parks, and anything fun and exciting! I also love love love to play games—it's the competitor in me, I guess!

Where is your favorite place to go with your girlfriends?
We have fun everywhere we go... although the day before we get together I always have to rest my stomach muscles in preparation for all the laughter!

Lindy Kleivo

Diane Richardson

Q and A

People may be surprised to know...
How energetically I search the globe acquiring the most beautiful and out-of-the-ordinary antique pieces.

What or who inspired you to start your business?
When I was a little girl, my grandmother showed me a gold heart-shaped signet ring, made by her grandfather from a gold nugget from the 1849 California gold rush.

Who is your role model or mentor?
Diana Vreeland, former editor of *Vogue*, who made elegance a state of mind and glamour attainable for every woman.

How do you spend your free time?
I'm an avid reader and a lover of Brazilian jazz. For fun, I travel the world hiking, kayaking, camping, and exploring the great outdoors.

What is your indulgence?
I have a hard time passing up any unusual antique needlecase—especially intricately carved ivory ones. They're my favorite.

THE GOLD HATPIN

125 N Marion St, Oak Park, 708.445.0610
goldhatpin.com

Dazzling. Addictive. Delicious.
The Gold Hatpin is a gem of a shop specializing in fine antique and estate jewelry, heirloom diamond engagement rings, ladies' and gentlemen's accessories, and extraordinary, vintage "paste with taste." Owned by Diane Richardson, the ever-changing collection spans centuries and includes: Georgian, Victorian, Deco, Art Nouveau and Arts and Crafts jewelry, whimsical bakelite, and vintage Mexican and designer sterling silver.

GRAY WELLNESS

300 N Canal St, Chicago, 347.393.2976
vgrayfitness.com, Twitter: @victoriadgray

Fun. Inspiring. Invaluable.

Fitness coach, coauthor of *Kettlebells, Strength Training for Power and Grace*, and owner of Gray Wellness, Victoria Gray is a certified athletic trainer, strength and conditioning coach, kettlebell instructor, and post-rehabilitation and pre/post-natal specialist. After 10 years of working with athletes, dancers, and fitness enthusiasts of all levels, Victoria believes that dedication and determination will help you accomplish any goal you may have.

Victoria D. Gray

Q and A

What are your most popular products or services?
Kettlebell and TRX instruction.

People may be surprised to know...
I was a Walt Disney World Dancer.

What or who inspired you to start your business?
A colleague and friend.

Who is your role model or mentor?
I do not have just one. I try to keep an open mind and learn from as many people as I can.

What business mistake have you made that you will not repeat?
Deciding to have a co-author on my book instead of writing it myself.

How do you spend your free time?
Meeting new people and being active.

Where is your favorite place to go with your girlfriends?
New York City.

Q and A

What are your most popular products or services?
Organic onesies with unique and fun graphics, gDiapers, Sophie the giraffe, glass baby bottles, Sigg bottles, and Envirosax.

Who is your role model or mentor?
For Heather, it's her father, who established his own successful business. For Tina, it's her mother, an 85-year-old spitfire!

What business mistake have you made that you will not repeat?
Early on, we definitely ordered too deep in some items, and that is just something we have to keep in check, even now.

How do you spend your free time?
For both of us, it's photography and artwork. We also enjoy cooking classes, antiquing and escaping from the city periodically.

What is your indulgence?
Spa days and sleeping in late.

Heather Muenstermann
and Christina Isperduli

GREEN GENES

5111 N Clark St, Chicago, 773.944.9250
green-genes.com

Sustainable. Organic. Eco-friendly.
Green Genes is an organic and eco-friendly boutique specializing in green goodies for kiddos and grown-ups, too! Since opening its doors in March 2008, Green Genes has been providing local, sustainable, and green products to neighborhood consumers and visitors alike. Here you'll find clothing, bath and body products, baby gear, stationery, and cards, as well as vintage and repurposed items.

HARMONY HAUS

Evanston, 773.677.6465
harmonyhaus.com, facebook.com/nichole.lovett

Scintillating. Efficient. Restorative.

Harmony Haus specializes in environmentally-conscious painting services both for residential and commercial interiors. At Harmony Haus, efficiency and minimizing waste—from the paints and materials used, to modes of transportation, and everything in between—are of the utmost importance. But creating surroundings and spaces that people love, while being kind to both health and the environment, is their passion.

Nichole Lovett

Q and A

What are your most popular products or services?
Beautiful painting and unique color consultations, custom murals, and natural plaster applications.

People may be surprised to know...
I commute by bike and trailer with all materials in tow to the majority of job sites. People are often amazed that I do nearly all of the work myself.

What business mistake have you made that you will not repeat?
I once agreed to give someone an estimate over the phone before seeing their space, and it ended up being a complete nightmare. It happened early on but it ended up being a great learning experience.

What is your indulgence?
I look forward to the manicure and pedicure I get at the end of each large job. It's well deserved after so much hard work.

Where is your favorite place to go with your girlfriends?
We get together for "girls' nights in" with wine and finger foods, and we make art or crafts together!

Laura Dixon

Q and A

What are your most popular products or services?
Private Pilates sessions with our staff of certified instructors. Individual attention is key in understanding the fundamentals of Pilates.

People may be surprised to know...
Anyone can do Pilates! We know how to modify exercises to make them beneficial for every body.

What or who inspired you to start your business?
I wanted to find a way to balance my creative side with my business-minded side. Teaching regularly, training instructors, and maintaining a close relationship with clients has allowed me to find a perfect balance.

What business mistake have you made that you will not repeat?
Having the "disease to please." It is simply impossible to please everybody all the time, so I have learned to put less pressure on myself.

How do you spend your free time?
Walking my dog, dinner with friends, taking yoga, reading, and shopping in local boutiques.

HARMONY MIND BODY FITNESS

1962 N Bissell, Chicago, 773.296.0263
harmonybody.com, Twitter: @harmonybody

Rejuvenating. Fun. Inspiring.
Harmony Mind Body Fitness, located in the heart of Lincoln Park, offers private, duet, and group sessions in Pilates, GYROTONIC®, and GYROKINESIS®. All of these forms of exercise and bodywork are changing the way people work out, as they find intelligent, fun exercise does exist! Harmony offers clients, from novice to athlete, a chance to find a more meaningful connection between mind and body as they move.

HELEN FICALORA

2014 N Halsted, Chicago, 773.883.2014
helenficalora.com

Beautiful. Elegant. Timeless.
Helen Ficalora showcases her unique collection of charms, chains, earrings, rings, and
bracelets in a beautiful jewel box setting. You can create your own signature necklace with
Helen's alphabet charms, or stack rings and layer necklaces for a glamorous look. Perfect as
a special gift or personal treat, Helen Ficalora's designs inspire beauty, love, and peace.

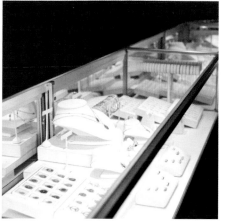

Helen Ficalora

Q and A

What are your most popular products or services?
Alphabet charms, flower rings, and earrings.

People may be surprised to know...
I ran a beach motel while building my jewelry business.

What or who inspired you to start your business?
Realizing that I needed to do what I
love and follow my passion.

Who is your role model or mentor?
My mother.

How do you spend your free time?
At the beach and with my family.

What is your indulgence?
Dark chocolate and diamonds.

Where is your favorite place to go with your girlfriends?
Karyn's Cooked on Wells.

115

HONEY

499 N Main St, Glen Ellyn, 630.469.0000
honeycafe.net

Modern. Comfort. Indulgence.
Honey is a full-service restaurant with a bright, modern appeal. You'll find bakery treats made from scratch by talented in-house bakers, fair-trade organic coffee roasted by Chicago's own Metropolis, and entrees made from the freshest ingredients, all local and organic whenever possible.

Elizabeth Janus

Q and A

What or who inspired you to start your business?
I was in a progressive cafe on vacation and thought,
"This is the kind of place Glen Ellyn needs."

Who is your role model or mentor?
Ina Garten, and my very fabulous friend, Kathy Keller.

What business mistake have you made
that you will not repeat?
We almost made the mistake of not having a fryer on
principle. It is so worth it to have our amazing fries!

How do you spend your free time?
Visiting new restaurants and supporting independent
businesses—where all the cool stuff can be discovered.

What is your indulgence?
Good Indian food and anything from our bakery.

Where is your favorite place to go with your girlfriends?
Their houses—they're all very creative
and wonderful cooks!

117

Charyl Witz

Q and A

What are your most popular products or services?
Dresses, handbags, and jewelry.

What or who inspired you to start your business?
My husband, Harry.

Who is your role model or mentor?
From the time I was a little girl I have always been interested in all things fashion.

What business mistake have you made that you will not repeat?
Location, location, location!

What is your indulgence?
A glass of fine wine.

How do you spend your free time?
Hanging out with my husband and our wonderful dogs, Angus and Olive.

Where is your favorite place to go with your girlfriends?
Trying the great restaurants of Chicago.

HUNNY BOUTIQUE

2027 N Damen Ave, Chicago, 773.292.1120
hunnyjewelry.com

Fashionable. Affordable. Comfortable.
Hunny Boutique blends clothing with jewelry for the perfect balance of casual, stylish, and comfortable dressing. You'll find a yin-yang approach to combining accessories and clothing, easily taking you from day to evening with the simple addition of the perfect jacket, earrings, or handbag.

INNOVATIVE ORTHODONTIC CENTERS

111 N Wabash Ave, Ste 1820, Chicago, 312.640.1760
55 S Main St, Ste 251, Naperville, 630.848.6960
1526 Il Route 59, Joliet, 815.436.8787
orthocenters.org, Twitter: @orthocenters

Innovative. Compassionate. Friendly.
Founded by Dr. Manal Ibrahim, a dual-trained specialist in prosthetic dentistry and orthodontics, Innovative Orthodontic Centers provides the most innovative orthodontic techniques currently available for patients ages 7 to 70+. As the sole practioner at Innovative, Dr. Ibrahim's passion for dentistry, as well as her loving approach towards her patients, sets her apart from the rest.

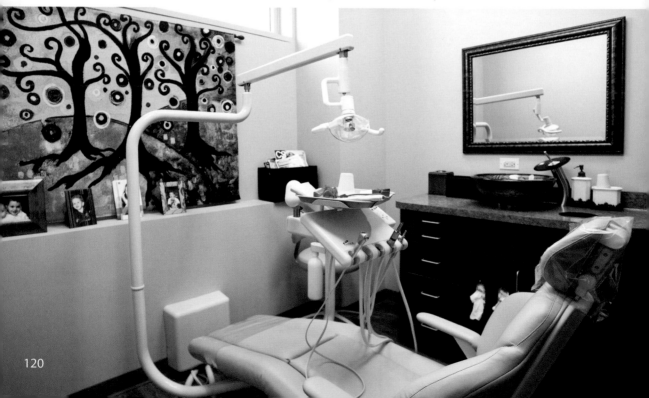

Dr. Manal Ibrahim

Q and A

What are your most popular products or services?
Clear braces and Invisalign.

People may be surprised to know...
That even 7-year-olds can have braces,
and the enhancement to their self esteem
and appearance is tremendous.

What or who inspired you to start your business?
It was incredibly difficult to work in other
businesses who didn't share the passion
of dentistry and love for patients.

Who is your role model or mentor?
If I could be even 1/4, the woman, friend, mother, and
wife my mother is, I would be so greatly enriched.

How do you spend your free time?
I spend every free second with my husband and sons.
I don't care what we do, as long as we're together.

What is your indulgence?
Everyone knows: sushi, shoes, and chai lattes!

Lauren Amerine (co-owner
Deborah Urban is not pictured)

 Q and A

What are your most popular products or services?
Bra fittings, wardrobe solutions, and
bridal/honeymoon gifts.

People may be surprised to know...
We carry the largest range of bra
sizes in Chicago (28-52, AA-K).

What or who inspired you to start your business?
The fact that we both have hard to find bra sizes
was an inspiration to open our doors and keep our
boutique stocked with bras in ALL sizes and styles.

Who is your role model or mentor?
Elizabeth Taylor in *Cat on a Hot Tin Roof* for
her sexiness, and Madonna for her staying
power, love of change, and reinvention.

What business mistake have you
made that you will not repeat?
Overindulging in too many amazing pieces for the
store before pinpointing our customer's needs.

ISABELLA FINE LINGERIE

840 W Armitage, Chicago, 773.281.2352
shopisabella.com, Twitter: @loveyourbras

Comfortable. Polished. Chic.
Isabella Fine Lingerie is the go-to-boutique for bra fittings in Chicago, featuring styles that are both classic and sexy. *InStyle*, *Lucky*, and *The Chicago Tribune* have all touted Isabella as the best bra fitters in the biz. Loungewear, wardrobe solutions, and skincare round out the well-edited selection, and make shopping at Isabella both luxurious and essential.

What business mistake have you made that you will not repeat?

"Not listening to what my customers say. It may not be easy to hear all of the feedback and comments, but it's priceless information"

Colette Gleeson, Colette

Q and A

What are your most popular products or services?
Complete planning and coordination
of the wedding day.

People may be surprised to know...
A wedding consultant can help save the client so
much money, even considering the added expense
of their service. The expertise they bring can be
invaluable, and their help with developing and
maintaining a realistic budget can mean the difference
between a pleasant experience and a nightmare!

How do you spend your free time?
I love reading, having dinner with friends and
family, and shopping for antiques with my
daughters, with whom I am extremely close.

What is your indulgence?
Anything sweet—especially wedding cake!

**Where is your favorite place to
go with your girlfriends?**
We always have fun trying great new restaurants.
We are so lucky to have so many in Chicago.

Joyce Westin Dunne

JOYCE WESTIN DUNNE WEDDING CONSULTANTS

Chicago, 773.975.9555
joycewestindunne.com

Attentive. Elegant. Timeless.
The weddings of Joyce Westin Dunne have set a new standard in elegant perfection. Her loving attention to detail and her singular focus on turning wedding desires into luxurious reality make her one of Chicago's most sought-after consultants. Her only goal is a perfect wedding.

Kayme Pumphrey

Q and A

What are your most popular products or services?
We work extensively with families that have part-time child care needs. We provide placements for occasional day/evening/weekend requests, overnight stays, full- and part-time nanny placements, and temporary and long-standing recurring jobs.

What or who inspired you to start your business?
K. Grace started as a hobby. I was working around the clock to help families I was unable to sit for, and one day I decided I should make something of it!

What business mistake have you made that you will not repeat?
I tend to focus on details versus the big picture. It is just who I am, but if at all possible, I try to keep things in perspective.

Where is your favorite place to go with your girlfriends?
My best girlfriend is my two-year-old daughter! We love to go to the zoo, out for lunch, to museums, parks, etc.

K. GRACE CHILDCARE

Chicago, 773.649.9149
kgracechildcare.com

Thorough. Convenient. Reputable.
K. Grace Childcare, a full-service agency that specializes in helping parents with part-time needs, was founded in 2002 with a commitment to placing exceptional childcare professionals based on the unique needs of each family. K. Grace is proud to have hundreds of qualified, young, educated, playful individuals who all fit the bill as the "best babysitter of all time." Professional standards, dedication to screening procedures, and a focus on providing quality service allow urban families flexibility and peace of mind.

KAREN ZAMBOS VINTAGE COUTURE

Chicago, 213.833.0093
karenzambos.com, Twitter: @karenzambos

Vintage-inspired. Fun. Easy.
Reinventing the allure of bohemian charm, Karen Zambos creates a fun and flirty collection that appeals to the confident and carefree spirit. As a child, Karen was inspired by the originality and comfort of vintage designs, and created a line that successfully fills the gap in the fashion market for vintage couture.

Q and A

Karen Zambos

What are your most popular products or services?
Every aspect of the company is flourishing,
especially dresses, belts, and bags.

People may be surprised to know...
I started my company because I was in debt.

What or who inspired you to start your business?
My success is attributed to believing in my
work and taking everything one step at a time.
Tracey Ross is credited for the push forward.

What business mistake have you made
that you will not repeat?
Overcutting fabrics.

How do you spend your free time?
Dinner with friends and research for happily dressing
confident, sexy, and playful women worldwide
in vintage clothing, with a modern twist.

Where is your favorite place to go with your girlfriends?
It doesn't matter where we are when we are all together!

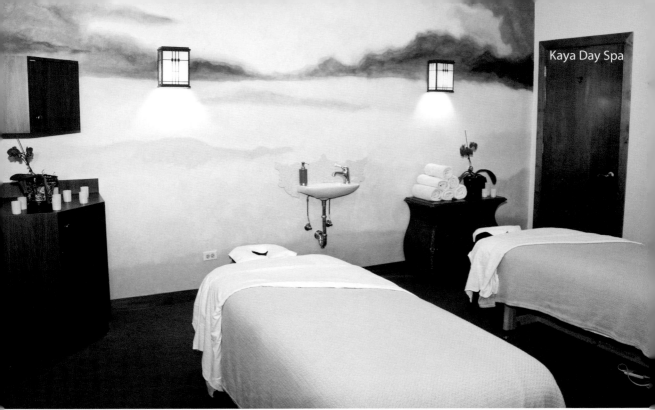

Kaya Day Spa

KAYA DAY SPA

112 N May St, Chicago, 312.243.5292
kayadayspa.com

ARISTA FOODS

112 N May St, Chicago, 312.239.2873
aristafoodschicago.com

Natural. Zen. Retreat.
When you step into Kaya Day Spa you are entering serenity. With 10,000 square feet of relaxation at your service and tailor-made treatments for both men and women, Kaya has the perfect recipe for indulgence.
Fresh. Fun. Delicious.
Arista Foods has a decadent selection of homemade foods in the deli, and hundreds of interesting and delicious wines, as well as everyday items that every household needs.

Q and A

What are your most popular products or services?
Jurlique and Sonya Dakar facials at Kaya Day Spa, wine, and anything in our deli case at Arista Foods.

People may be surprised to know...
I'm from an island in Greece called Ikaria where I was once in a band called Afromind (for a day).

What is your indulgence?
Traveling!

What or who inspired you to start your business?
While getting a manicure at another spa, it hit me. I can do this. I want to do this. I can do this better.

What business mistake have you made
that you will not repeat?
None of my mistakes have been tragic, but I do not plan on doing them again.

How do you spend your free time?
At the spa getting services.

Maria Sakoutis

Arista Foods

Arista Foods

Kaya Day Spa

133

KEE2CREATIVITY

Chicago, 708.932.2189
kee2creativity.com, Twitter: @kee2creativity, facebook.com/kee2creativity

Innovative. Chic. Trendy.
Kee2Creativity is a blossoming invitation and graphic design boutique boasting a signature
line of custom invitations and chic stationery, as well as a drool-inducing baby clothing
collection. Full-scale graphic capabilities allow us to meet virtually every design need, including
eye-catching designs for small and corporate businesses—all with an added flair!

 *Q* and *A*

People may be surprised to know...
I create all invitations from start to finish. From invitation concept and design, selecting the perfect papers, ribbons, and other embellishments, to assembling them one-by-one by hand. All of this ensures our clients' guests will receive a well-crafted, luxe masterpiece—one they'll want to save long after the party is over!

What business mistake have you made that you will not repeat?
Not believing in my gift and trying to fit into the norm. Trusting in my creative vision sets me apart and allows me to create uninhibitedly.

How do you spend your free time?
When it exists, I am relaxing, reading *HOW* or *Glamour* magazines, hanging out with loved ones, and cultivating my children's passions.

What is your indulgence?
All things paper, candles, hot baths, traveling, banana pudding, fashion, and shoes!

Arkeelaus Sherman

Kathryn Hudson

Q and A

What are your most popular products or services?
Our bra fitting service is very popular. We offer more than 20 years of fitting experience. It's the favorite part of our job; helping women feel beautiful, comfortable, and confident.

People may be surprised to know...
We offer unique bridal and home bra-fitting parties. And we have a sister store in Cincinnati's Hyde Park Square.

Where is your favorite place to go with your girlfriends?
There are so many fun restaurants in Glen Ellyn where we like to go to talk, laugh, connect, and encourage each other. Girlfriend time is so important!

Who is your role model or mentor?
My mom and dad. They both had their own businesses while I was growing up, and I've always admired their dedication, work ethic, and entrepreneurial spirit.

KNICKERS OF GLEN ELLYN

492 N Main St, Glen Ellyn, 630.469.BRAS
knickersofglenellyn.blogspot.com, Twitter: @knickersofGE, facebook.com/knickersofglenellyn

Feminine. Saucy. Sophisticated.
An upscale intimate apparel boutique, Knickers of Glen Ellyn offers a lovely selection of personal care items, fun girlfriend gifts, and luxurious lingerie—from comfy and cozy, to sexy and sophisticated. For a different kind of girls' get-together, have Knickers come to your house for a home bra-fitting party! Their personal service and luxe fabrics are sure to make Knickers one of your favorite shopping destinations.

KOROS

1039 W Lake St, Chicago, 312.738.0155
shopkoros.com

Unique. Fabulous. Fun.
Koros is truly one of Chicago's hidden gems. A unique, one-of-a kind approach to fashion and style has clients coming back for more. With a trend setting eye and innate sense of style Kristen Skordilis scours the US and Europe for amazing collections and accessories that are sure to please. Koros is the joy of style.

Kristen Skordilis

Q and A

What are your most popular products or services?
Personal styling appointments are
my clients' best kept secret!

What or who inspired you to start your business?
My dear family, friends, and clients who
couldn't get enough of my styling services.
And cool finds from around the globe.

Who is your role model or mentor?
My mother... always!

**What business mistake have you made
that you will not repeat?**
Trying to do everything yourself. It's not possible.

How do you spend your free time?
Traveling, cooking, photography, movies, and of course
researching designers and trying to find their agents.

Where is your favorite place to go with your girlfriends?
My kitchen, to whip up something new and delicious!

Lisa Kulisek

Q and A

What are your most popular products or services?
As people are thinking more about the planet, renovations are gaining status. Small changes with big impact save the environment!

People may be surprised to know...
Becoming an architect takes time. Most architects do not build a building of their own design before age 50.

What or who inspired you to start your business?
Every woman entrepreneur I have ever met (including my mom) has inspired me, but my husband gave me a supportive push.

How do you spend your free time?
With my family: singing, gardening, cooking.

What is your indulgence?
Sleep and hot tea (I am mother to a toddler!)

Where is your favorite place to go with your girlfriends?
Millennium Park.

KULISEK P.C.

1260 W Lexington St, Chicago, 312.738.2187
kulisekpc.com

Urban. Honest. Intelligent.
Kulisek P.C. is the Chicago architecture firm founded in 2008 by Lisa Kulisek, AIA. Lisa's widely varied project experience includes commercial, institutional, and residential project types. These range in size from small porch renovations to a large public museum. Lisa loves the variety and challenges that each project presents and is continually inspired by her clients. Every space has a story to tell.

LACQUER INTERIOR DESIGN

Chicago, 773.405.6548
lacquerinteriordesign.com

Innovative. Resourceful. Approachable.
Lacquer Interior Design offers a full range of services for both commercial and residential projects, for a wide range of clients with varying interests, needs, and budgets. Lacquer founder, Jen Hankee, encourages her clients to tap into and expand their vision, helping them achieve great style and function, while creating a space that reflects their own passions and personalities.

Jen Hankee

Q and A

What are your most popular products or services?
Conceptual design and development, space planning, fixture and finish selections, furniture and fabric selections, renovations, construction document development, and project management.

People may be surprised to know...
I grew up in Oregon and Alaska, and have been influenced by Northwest style, ease, design, and landscape. The first house I lived in made an impact as I watched my parents remodel. Each nook and detail is still a clear vision in my mind, and I would love to own it again some day!

What business mistake have you made that you will not repeat?
Working in a way that Sundays are filled with anxiety, Mondays are dreaded, and you miss the middle of the week because you are only waiting for Friday.

How do you spend your free time?
Sharing life's little pleasures with friends and family, or exploring corners of the world in search of the extraordinary.

 **Q and A**

What are your most popular products or services?
Ladysmith jewelry's most popular adornments are
made from vintage chandelier crystals. Ladysmith
Jewelry studio is also known for re-designing
grandma vintage necklace or old wedding
rings into new contemporary adornments.

People may be surprised to know...
My second passion in life is teaching. I
currently hold a faculty position at the
School of the Art Institute of Chicago.

What or who inspired you to start your business?
I was inspired to start my business as a way
to combine my passion and desire to have
a career that I love. My goal is to adorn the
world one beautiful person at a time.

How do you spend your free time?
Biking, preparing raw foods, and taking raw food chef
classes. I am also an educator in the jewelry field and
am inspired to teach others to find their creative voice.

Amy Butts

LADYSMITH JEWELRY STUDIO

5052 N Leavitt, Chicago, 773.895.8806
ladysmithjewelry.com

Vintage. Reinvented. Stylish.
Amy Butts, a Chicago-based metalsmith and jewelry artist and owner of Ladysmith Jewelry Studio, gives voice to the found objects she fashions into her striking designs. Ladysmith jewelry is available in boutiques and galleries throughout the Chicago area.

LARA MILLER

Chicago, 773.296.4442
laramiller.net, Twitter: @laramiller

Sultry. Sophisticated. Endlessly variable.
Lara Miller is influenced by Chicago's architectural and cultural landscape. Fashioned from eco-friendly fibers such as organic cotton, hand-loomed bamboo, hemp, and vegan silk, Lara's modular designs are created with a playful geometry that connects to the personalities of the women who wear them. Garments can be wrapped, reversed, and, most distinguishably, flipped, to reveal an entirely different look. Acknowledging the impact that we all have on our environment, Lara aspires to preserve and respect our earth in every way possible.

Lara Miller

Q and A

What are your most popular products or services?
My flip sweaters—especially the Kelleigh tank—can be worn as a dress, flipped as a sweater, or wrapped as a scarf.

How do you spend your free time?
When I'm not Lara Miller "the designer," I'm Lara Miller "Executive Director of the Chicago Fashion Incubator." When I can find free time, I run marathons, dance in grocery store aisles with my husband, listen to Pat and Ron CUBS radio, and drink bubble tea (in the summer) and hot chocolate (in the winter).

What is your indulgence?
Molly's vegan cupcakes! YUM!

Who is your role model or mentor?
I have too many to list. I have been so lucky to have been helped by so many people, and am incredibly grateful.

What business mistakes have you made that you will not repeat?
Not understanding how to put overhead into my budget when I first began—ouch!

Lauren Lein

Q and A

What are your most popular products or services?
Custom suits and cocktail dresses, and free styling consultations with design selection.

People may be surprised to know...
That my platinum blond hair really is natural!

What or who inspired you to start your business?
Professional women who dressed frumpy, dumpy, and styleless 20 years ago. I wanted to lend a touch of "feminine chic" to modern business attire.

How do you spend your free time?
Having colorful adventures with my kids, hubby, and friends.

What is your indulgence?
Shoes, food, museums, and travel. You only live once!

Where is your favorite place to go with your girlfriends?
Trying out new places for cocktails and dinner, or catching the latest new film.

LAUREN LEIN DESIGN

Chicago, 312.527.1714
laurenlein.com

Creative. Flamboyant. Sassy.
Lauren's signature style is recognized by eclectic blends of luxurious fabrics and textures. Each piece is complete with her artful touch—feathers, beading, fur trim, a simple bow or hand-made flower. These avant-garde couture pieces, as well as her classic ready-to-wear collections, have been commissioned by Nordstrom, Marshall Field's, Macy's, and boutiques nationwide.

LE DRESS

1741 W Division St, Chicago, 773.697.9899
ledresschicago.com

Fun. Flirty. Chic.
Conceived by sisters-in-law and trend-setters Eva and Robyn Anderson, this "dress only" destination offers customers special services, from complimentary wardrobe styling to an in-house seamstress, and a stylist-kit-to-go. Le Dress carries more than 50 lines—from both established and emerging designers—to fit every budget, with day, cocktail, and career dresses ranging from $40 to $500. Le Dress also carries various accessories and essential undergarments to complete any look.

Eva and Robyn Anderson

Q and A

People may be surprised to know...
We offer "le Dress Me Chic" private party packages,
perfect for sipping and shopping with your fav ladies.

What or who inspired you to start your business?
The inspiration for le Dress came from our collective
experiences living and shopping in some of the
fashion capitals of the world, Paris and New York.

What business mistake have you made
that you will not repeat?
Thinking that you can please everyone! We
have to be true to ourselves and our vision.

How do you spend your free time?
Relaxing with our significant others and our dogs.

What is your indulgence?
Anything chocolate, a great glass of
wine, and a fabulous pair of shoes.

Where is your favorite place to go with your girlfriends?
Anywhere outside in the summer with great cocktails!

151

THE LEFT BANK JEWELRY & UNIQUITIES

1155 W Webster Ave, Chicago, 773.929.7422
leftbankjewelry.com, Twitter: @leftbankjewelry, facebook.com/leftbankjewelry

Charming. Fanciful. Feminine.
The Left Bank is a Parisian-inspired boutique known for an incredible collection of unique jewelry and accessories. For a combination of vintage and modern bridal charm, brides flock to The Left Bank for its extraordinary selection of headpieces, veils, and the Midwest's largest wedding shoe salon. Wonderful gifts, home décor, and small indulgences adorn this magical Lincoln Park boutique.

Susan Metropoulos

What are your most popular products or services?
Our exclusive lines of jewelry made in France, lovely wedding jewelry, and a tremendous collection of bridal shoes.

What or who inspired you to start your business?
My grandmother Genevieve, who was always adorned in gorgeous accessories, which I now proudly own, and, most importantly, wear! Her home was like walking into a jewelry box filled with treasures and beautiful things. In the 1950s, she created a decadent gift boutique within our family's hardware store, and I was the chief duster!

How do you spend your free time?
Playing tennis, grocery shopping, cooking, and playing with my adorable Pug, Sushie Lee.

What is your indulgence?
A quiet bubble bath with candles and a glass of vino.

Where is your favorite place to go with your girlfriends?
As a perpetual hostess, I love spending time with friends at our respective homes, opening up some wine or bubbly, and sharing great bites.

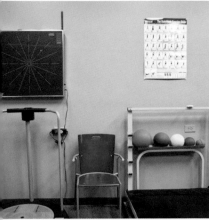

Michele A. Kehrer PT, DPT, ATC

Q and A

What are your most popular products or services?
Physical therapy and vestibular rehabilitation
for dizziness and balance disorders.

People may be surprised to know...
I am a two time breast cancer survivor.

What or who inspired you to start your business?
I remember being 5 or 6 years old knowing I
wanted to open my own business. After college I
assisted in opening several physical therapy clinics
and decided I could do this better on my own.

Who is your role model or mentor?
Elliot Shear from SCORE mentored me through the
entire process of opening my business, from writing
my business plan to present day marketing.

How do you spend your free time?
Running. Volunteering for my favorite
charities, Imerman Angels and Bright Pink.
Providing volunteer physical therapy/athletic
training services for a local high school.

LIFESTYLE PHYSICAL THERAPY & BALANCE CENTER

3130 N Lincoln Ave, Chicago, 773.525.5200
balancechicago.com, Twitter: @balancechicago

Dynamic. Innovative. Authentic.
With an unprecedented success rate of over 90 percent of patients experiencing a marked decrease in symptoms within four to eight weeks, LifeStyle Physical Therapy & Balance Center is unique among its peers. Offering a mixture of traditional and innovative new therapies, LifeStyle Physical Therapy & Balance Center provides comprehensive evaluations, and specializes in the treatment of dizziness and balance disorders.

LISA ROSEN JEWELRY

Chicago, 773.502.9570
lisarosen.com

Personal. Fresh. Boundless.

Combining her love of fashion, family, and community inspired Lisa Rosen to design and craft jewelry that is feminine and timeless. Her passion evolved into a business that allows her to spend time with her son, bring beauty to others, and give back to the community. Lisa Rosen Jewelry has given more than $50,000 in gifts and contributions to local and national charities.

Lisa Rosen

Q and A

What are your most popular products or services?
The Flirt collection. People are attracted
to the delicacy and sophistication.

People may be surprised to know...
I hand-pick each stone. They come from all over the
world and are the inspiration for each design.

What or who inspired you to start your business?
I wanted to show my son how to weave creativity, family
and community to create a successful and happy life.

What is your indulgence?
A great massage, a hot shower, chocolate, and
music that moves me to dance in my underwear!

Where is your favorite place to go with your girlfriends?
Anywhere I don't have to cook and can
hear some great Chicago blues!

How do you spend your free time?
Cheering on my son at his hockey,
football, and baseball games.

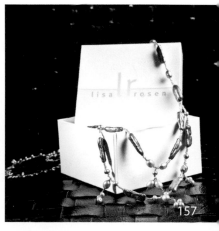

LOVE, LULU MAE

Chicago
lovelulumae.com, Twitter: @LoveLuluMae

Fierce. Feminine. Fashionable.
Love, Lulu Mae is Chicago's ARTcessories for the modern woman with a vintage soul. Featuring couture hair accessories, designer Agnes B. Miles models every piece she creates after the elegant styles of the women of the 1930s and 1940s. From stylish clips to more elaborate headbands and bridal creations, Love, Lulu Mae joins fine femininity and fierce fashion for the modern woman.

Q and A

Agnes B. Miles

What are your most popular products or services?
Our "Viva La Frida" headband, composed of
various textured flowers in assorted colors.

People may be surprised to know...
I majored in musical theatre performance.

What or who inspired you to start your business?
My amazing friends and family.

Who is your role model or mentor?
My sister Tina, my mother, my husband,
and my friend, Janelle.

How do you spend your free time?
Taking my two Boston Terriers on walks with my
husband, as well as mini-getaways with them, too!

What is your indulgence?
I absolutely love Vosges Chocolates.
They are my favorite indulgence.

Where is your favorite place to go with your girlfriends?
Shopping on the Mag Mile, of course!

M.GO FASHION SALON

1754 W Division St, Chicago, 773.772.2772
mgofashion.com, Twitter: @dynamic72

Creative. Innovative. Affordable.

At M.GO Fashion Salon, three levels of fashion, beauty, and music come together in one location. At this late-hours, one-stop shop, both men and women can buy an outfit, get a haircut, get makeup done, get a temporary tattoo, hear fresh music, and then go out for a fun evening on Division Street's trendy strip!

Michelle and Melissa Gomez

Q and A

What are your most popular products or services?
Our stylish apparel is always a hit. We offer complimentary consultations to create a new style for you. Our no-chip manicures and pedicures are a must. The special polish goes on a natural nail and will last for up to three weeks. Our men's haircuts were voted CitySearch's "Best Haute Cuts 2008."

People may be surprised to know...
We alter any garment that may not fit, or change the design on any previously owned garment.

How do you spend your free time?
Michelle likes to make home-cooked meals by finding new recipes from friends, books, and our abuela's (grandma's) great dishes. Melissa likes to research new possibilities for the business and eat Michelle's tasty food!

What business mistake have you made that you will not repeat?
Not taking risks. Reinventing yourself and your business is a must. Don't doubt your ideas, even when they don't work out.

MAXINE

712 N Rush St, Chicago, 312.751.1511
maxinesalon.com, Twitter: @maxinesalon

Chic. Progressive. Friendly.
Maxine is a top Chicago salon just steps away from Michigan Avenue. Progressive and
chic with a first-rate reputation, the friendly, nurturing staff dedicates themselves to
delivering the best, most up-to-date haircuts, hair color, and treatments available.

Maxine Kroll

Q and A

What are your most popular products or services?
Extraordinary haircuts, Balayage coloring, keratin smoothing treatments, personalized facials, Brazilian bikini waxing, and spa pedicures.

What or who inspired you to start your business?
My clients.

Who is your role model or mentor?
My husband who never stops believing in tomorrows.

What business mistake have you made that you will not repeat?
Not trusting my gut.

How do you spend your free time?
Escaping to Cabo San Lucas.

What is your indulgence?
Yoga, as many days a week as I can fit it in.

Where is your favorite place to go with your girlfriends?
On my balcony, overlooking the Rush Street buzz.

What business mistake have you made that you will not repeat?

"*Standing still is not an option. You must always be considering what is next.*"

Jennifer Velarde, 1154 LILL STUDIO

Q and A

What are your most popular products or services?
Ruffled scarves, halfies, and two-colored capelets.

People may be surprised to know...
I work directly with Mayu's artisans in
Peru. We love dancing to Andean Huayno
music and baking American desserts.

Who is your role model or mentor?
My dad. He encourages me to think outside the
box, take risks, and ask the right questions.

What business mistake have you
made that you will not repeat?
I sent Mayu samples to a large corporation
who wanted to make an order. Instead,
they copied and sold them.

What is your indulgence?
A nice pair of designer jeans, a hand-crafted
belt buckle, and a Dairy Queen Blizzard.

Kate Robertson

MAYU

Chicago, 847.363.7186
shopmayu.com

Socially-conscious. Hand-knit. Chic.
Mayu sells one-of-a-kind, handmade accessories that are knit by a group of female artisans in the Andes Mountains of Peru. All of their products are created with the highest-quality, eco-friendly, alpaca fiber. Knitting for Mayu has given these women an opportunity to better provide for themselves and their families. Mayu's products are stylish and sophisticated, and always make a great addition to any outfit!

Cynthia Kallile

Q and A

What are your most popular products or services?
Everyone loves The Mother Loaf—our version of the classic topped with Yukon Smashers. We always encourage everyone to enjoy our other inspired creations, like El Loafo Del Fuego and No Buns About It Burger Loaf. Yum!

People may be surprised to know...
With a bit of creativity and a sense of adventure, some of the most basic ingredients can blend together to become truly marvelous meatloaves.

What or who inspired you to start your business?
I've loved being around food since I was a little girl, learning from my mom who was the best and most fearless cook I knew. But the real inspiration for starting my business came from a tiny, but persistent voice inside of me. I knew I had something unique, and despite words of caution from many, I stayed the course and opened The Meatloaf Bakery.

How do you spend your free time?
I love to cook, roam markets and grocery stores, and enjoy friends, family, and must-see TV.

THE MEATLOAF BAKERY

2464 N Clark St, Chicago, 773.698.6667
themeatloafbakery.com

Adventurous. Creative. Delicious.
Imagine the taste and aroma of your favorite meatloaf. Whether it's a delicious twist on the comforting loaf you grew up with, or a variation you never imagined, The Meatloaf Bakery has it all. This one-of-a-kind shop features ready-to-go meatloaf cupcakes, meatloaf pastries, and exclusive bite-size Loafies. Eight scrumptious recipes are available every day, including The Mother Loaf, Herby Turkey, and A Wing and a Prayer.

MEMORIES WOW!

Mary V. Gutowski-Hazzard

Q and A

What are your most popular products or services?
Digital photobooks and film/vhs conversions to DVD.

People may be surprised to know...
Only about 10 percent of photos that are
captured are actually printed or archived.

**What was the inspiration or motivation
behind starting your business?**
The need for an easy, affordable way to manage all
of the photos and videos that accompany life.

Who is your role model or mentor?
Any entrepreneur mom who is successful in business,
motherhood, and marriage. Balancing all three is tough!

**What mistake have you made in your
business that you will not repeat?**
Underestimating the time, effort, and resources
that go into launching a business.

MUDD FLEUR

1800 W Lake St, Chicago, 312.337.6833
muddfleur.com, Twitter: @muddfleur

Chic, stylish and distinctive
Mudd Fleur is a luxury, floral design studio dedicated to the highest-quality, lush floral arrangements. Using exotic florals flown in daily from all around the world, Mudd Fleur is devoted to creating arrangements that make an impression—the key reason that high-profile clients, such as well-known boutiques and top hotels in Chicago, look to Mudd to adorn their spaces.

Maria Petrides, Katherine
Benetatos, and Maria Benetatos

Q and A

People may be surprised to know…
Mudd Fleur is a division of Northern Greenhouses,
a full-service floral and event design company.
The partnership has allowed Mudd to take on
larger scale weddings and special events.

What or who inspired you to start your business?
Our desire to own our own business, and our mutual
love for floral and high-style design. It was a "no-brainer"!

Who is your role model or mentor?
Our parents. They taught us the keys to success: hard
work, determination, and truly loving what you do!

What is your indulgence?
It's unanimous … spa treatments! What
can we say,? We're girly girls!

Where is your favorite place to go with your girlfriends?
We absolutely love escaping to NoMi at the
Park Hyatt. The view is breathtaking!

MULBERRY & ME

2019 W Division, Chicago, 773.952.7551
mulberryandme.com, Twitter: @mulberryandme

Chic. Stylish. Friendly.

Mulberry & Me is a reflection of Jana Zacek's philosophy that your clothes should fall into one of two categories: a great basic that is in heavy rotation in your wardrobe, or an item that is so special that you just have to have it. Sprinkle in a comfortable environment where you receive honest feedback from a fun stylist. The boutique is simple, and offers fabulous clothes and friendship.

Jana Zacek

Q and A

What or who inspired you to start your business?
Living on Mulberry Street with my boyfriend in the NoLita neighborhood of New York City inspired me to start my boutique. NoLita attracts shoppers seeking independent boutiques with unique merchandise in a cozy neighborhood atmosphere, and that is what I have recreated in the Wicker Park neighborhood of Chicago. Even more important than the inspiration, though, is the continued encouragement and support of my boyfriend!

Who is your role model or mentor?
My mom is just *the* ultimate role model. She owned a coffee shop in our neighborhood when I was growing up. She taught me about running your business with love. That is the base of everything.

What is your indulgence?
A glass of red wine, a good read, and unwinding in the bathtub. Preferably all three at the same time!

How do you spend your free time?
It's not so much how I spend it, but rather with whom do I spend it. I make sure to spend it with my loved ones.

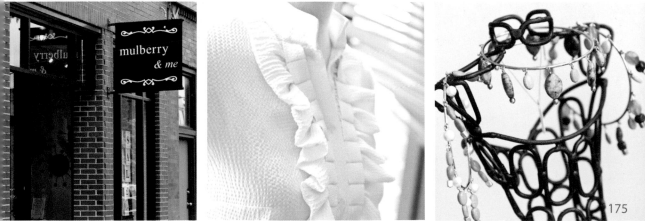

Carrie Nahabedian

Q and A

What are your most popular products or services?
Our whole roasted and dressed ranch squab with foie gras, scented with Armenian rose petal marmalade and licorice root. Also, the Great Lakes whitefish with Spence Farm wheat berries and butter-poached Maine lobster; and, at lunch, our famous Southern fried chicken salad, or the lacquered pork belly with roasted beets and 3 Sisters garden white corn polenta.

People may be surprised to know...
That we have a great bar and lounge menu that is available from 5:30 pm, as well as a beautiful list of aperitif specialty drinks.

What is your indulgence?
I love a great lunch. Long lunches, followed by shopping and then drinks and possibly an early dinner ... I am a big fan of a great facial. If I really have time, a day in the sun and a big swimming pool is my idea of heaven.

NAHA

500 N Clark St, Chicago, 312.321.6242
naha-chicago.com, Twitter: @cnaha

Seasonal. Inspired. Mediterranean.
NAHA is a chef-driven, architecturally-designed restaurant that features American cuisine with
Mediterranean influence. Their menus are heavily influenced by the season, and they support the many
local farmers and artisans of the Midwest community. Their menus, service style, and natural ambiance
reflect the focus and passion of Chef Carrie Nahabedian and her cousin and partner, Michael Nahabedian.

NAME YOUR DESIGN

Naperville, 630.536.8501
nameyourdesign.com, Twitter: @designfiles

Modern. Simple. Unique.
Name your design is home to a line of personalized wall art for the modern family. The clean and simple designs are sweet enough for babies—but chic enough for big kids and adults too! Name your design's canvas and fine art prints are the perfect compliment to any room in your house.

Stacy Amoo-Mensah

 Q and A

What are your most popular products or services?
Our canvas prints have been a huge hit among young, urban parents and their cool kids.

People may be surprised to know...
I am a completely self-taught designer. I actually majored in education and taught kindergarten for several years before branching out on my own.

What or who inspired you to start your business?
I was craving unique art for my son's room. I couldn't find what I wanted, so I made it myself!

Who is your role model or mentor?
My mom! I grew up watching her build an interior design business from scratch. I was lucky enough to inherit some of her ambition.

How do you spend your free time?
I don't have much! However, I do enjoy my workouts and the down time with my husband and three beautiful boys.

Q and A

Cindy Rudman

What are your most popular products or services?
Invitations and stationery for every occasion and embroidered gifts, especially the last minute kind.

What or who inspired you to start your business?
I've loved paper since I received my first set of personalized stationery for my 8th birthday.

Who is your role model or mentor?
My dad who died last year. I think how he would handle any situation before deciding how to proceed.

What business mistake have you made that you will not repeat?
Allowing a client to pay upon delivery. Her wedding was cancelled, and she decided she did not need to pay for her invites.

How do you spend your free time?
With my husband and two kids, but I attempt to get to the gym and hang out with friends.

NOTEWORTHY

1440 N Kingsbury, Ste 119, Chicago, 312.932.9565
noteworthynotes.com, Twitter: @noteworthynotes, facebook.com/noteworthynotes

Custom. Unique. Happy.
Located in Lincoln Park, Noteworthy is a hidden gem specializing in custom invitations, stationery, and gifts for all of life's milestones. Well known for incredibly fast turnaround on in-house printing and embroidered gifts—as well as friendly smiles and quality customer service—make all your occasions Noteworthy!

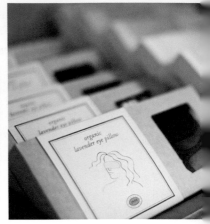

Nourhy Chiriboga

Q and A

People maybe surprised to know...
My age, that I have a twin brother (and yes, we do share feelings!), and that I survived a near death experience which prompted me into the work I do now.

What is your indulgence?
Sleeping late on Sundays, eating an excellent piece of Vosges Chocolate, and getting monthly microdermabrasion facials.

What was the inspiration or motivation behind starting your business?
NOW Studio is my response to what I learned in my own holistic healing experience--in seeking safer, natural therapies that offered an alternative to drugs for pain relief and stress. When I started working, I felt most spas didn't take time to understand an individual; they often lacked knowledge of the spiritual/energetic healing components that help one become more empowered to heal their health issues. I really wanted people to leave feeling like they got so much more then what they thought they came in for.

NOW STUDIO FOR HOLISTIC WELLNESS

2141 W Webster, Chicago, 773.276.5278
nourhy.com, Twitter: @nourhy

Restorative. Meditative. Holistic healing.
Charming, cozy NOW (Nourhy on Webster) Studio inspires their clients to let go of their everyday stresses and allow the holistic benefits of reflexology, craniosacral and intuitive massages relax the nervous system and unblock restrictions in the body. Owner Nourhy Chiriboga enjoys helping people let go of stressful thoughts, leaving them feeling positive, empowered, and eager to take better care of themselves.

OLIVE OWL ORGANICS

1101 Lake St, Suite 110, Oak Park, 708.383.SOAP (7627)
oliveowlorganics.com, Twitter: @oliveowl

Organic. Funky. Fun.
Olive Owl Organics is a natural, eco-friendly, Oak Park-based body shop infused with a funky flair. Their specialty is handmade signature soap bursting with herbs, essential oil goodness, and flower fun. Breathe in, exhale, and relax. Try samples at the "faucet" bar! Other unique goodies include: body care, funky eco bags, baby basics and more, all made with peace and love.

Cynthia
Orrico

Q and A

What are your most popular products or services?
Lavender citrus bar soap, peppermint eucalyptus
salt scrub, cocoa mint lip balm, citrus bath bombs,
and sandalwood and sage soy candles.

What or who inspired you to start your business?
I woke up one morning, looked at my husband and said,
"I think I am going to make soap." The rest is history!

Who is your role model or mentor?
My mom is proud and creative, and always provides
unconditional love. She is my support tree. My hubby
Pete is my biggest fan, and never lets me give up.

**What business mistake have you made
that you will not repeat?**
Don't wait on an idea because you think you do
not have the time. Someone will beat you to it!

Where is your favorite place to go with your girlfriends?
A friend's house or backyard. Kick off the shoes,
have a few drinks and a bunch of laughs—
and maybe some cool dance moves.

185

ONE MIND BODY & BEING

2035 W Wabansia, Chicago, 773.360.1397
onemindbodybeing.com, Twitter: @1mindbodybeing

Rewarding. Attainable. Balanced.
Since opening in 2004, One Mind Body & Being has been motivating clients to develop and maintain an overall sense of wellness. Located in the heart of Bucktown, One accommodates a variety of clientele from all levels of fitness, including those with injury-recovery and physical therapy needs. Services include individual and group Pilates instruction, yoga, body-sculpting mat classes, boot camp, and rope burn.

Stacy Weinstein

Q and A

What or who inspired you to start your business?
Many years ago I was injured in a yoga class by an instructor and Pilates became part of my physical therapy. Not only did it help heal me, but I found my passion and calling to teach.

Who is your role model or mentor?
I am fortunate that I have the support and guidance, as well as entrepreneurial spirit, from both of my parents. Although I might not always agree, they have never steered me in the wrong direction.

What business mistake have you made that you will not repeat?
Two weeks in a row I slept through my alarm and missed a lesson with the same client. He warned me that the third time wouldn't be so charming.

What is your indulgence?
I love cookies and can justify eating any sweet that has some kind of nutritional content—peanut M&Ms, oatmeal cookies, and soy ice cream sandwiches.

PAIR CHOCOLATES

734 W Northwest Highway, Barrington, 847.277.7980
pairchocolates.com

Natural. Indulgent. Stylish.
Featuring primarily organic and all-natural gourmet chocolates from around the globe, Pair is the place to discover your chocolate muse! Whether you prefer to sample chocolate from Madagascar, Africa, or South and Central America, or attend a monthly chocolate-and-wine-pairing event, Pair Chocolates is the destination for chocolates in the northwest suburbs.

Pam Tichy

Q and A

What are your most popular products or services?
The organic chocolate truffles, bon-bons, and caramels, and the homemade hot chocolates.

What or who inspired you to start your business?
My husband and I were craving chocolate on vacation in Florida in Spring of 2008. We found a boutique very similar to what I had always pictured as the perfect shop. I spent over an hour just talking to the owner, and she told me she loved her job because "People come in happy and leave happier." I walked out saying to my husband that was the job I wanted. Five months later, Pair Chocolates opened to the public.

How do you spend your free time?
I have two boys, so most of my free time is with them, watching them play their favorite sports, or taking them traveling to broaden their horizons.

Where is your favorite place to go with your girlfriends?
The spa, of course! But I have a hard time not laughing in the ladies' lounge, where you're supposed to be silent!

Stacy Weitzman

Q and A

What are your most popular products or services?
Upon check-out, each item will be "gift-ready" with Peek-a-Boutique's charm. We have both edgy and sweet baby gifts, and super cool toddler clothing, too!

People may be surprised to know...
I really focus on the boy section, and spend an equal amount on boy and girl!

Who is your role model or mentor?
My friend, Randi, owner of Randoons in Winnetka, has been my mentor since the beginning. It is great to have a friend in the same business! We learn a lot from each other.

How do you spend your free time?
With my niece and nephew, going out to dinner with family and friends, antiquing, shopping, or going to see local live bands.

Where is your favorite place to go with your girlfriends?
Going out to dinner—especially tapas! Also, I love going to Chicago festivals in the summer and fall.

PEEK-A-BOUTIQUE

2750 Dundee Rd, Ste 6, Northbrook, 847.272.7133
peek-a-boutique.com, facebook.com/peekaboutique

Sweet. Edgy. Friendly.

Whether you need a baby gift or a new wardrobe for your own children, you're sure to find something unique and special at Peek-a-Boutique. Owner Stacy Weitzman hand-selects each item in her shop, many of which are made by local artists. Having just celebrated their four-year anniversary, Peek-a-Boutique looks forward to stylishly outfitting babies and children for many years to come.

Q and A

What are your most popular products or services?
Corporate event production and
meeting management.

People may be surprised to know...
Plan Ahead Events is part of a global conglomerate.

What or who inspired you to start your business?
I wanted to help organizations realize
their event marketing objectives.

Who is your role model or mentor?
Stephen Covey and Ray Kroc.

What business mistake have you
made that you will not repeat?
Supporting too many organizations.

How do you spend your free time?
With my husband and daughter.
They are truly amazing!

What is your indulgence?
Stand-up comedy.

Melissa
Wojcik

PLAN AHEAD EVENTS OF CHICAGO NAPERVILLE

2 Prudential Plaza, 180 N Stetson St, Ste 3500, Chicago, 312.268.5879
planaheadevents-naperville.com, Twitter: @PAEChicago, facebook.com/planaheadevents

Service-oriented. Detailed. Professional.
Through the use of strategic event marketing, Plan Ahead Events, helps clients grow and succeed, even in this tough economy. By managing face-to-face meetings and events for clients, Plan Ahead Events has helped numerous businesses increase sales and brand recognition, while saving money and providing peace of mind.

April Wilson

Q and A

What are your most popular products or services?
Our new photo engagement signature book is our most popular new product. We offer La-Vie and Graphi albums—the best in the industry.

Who is your role model or mentor?
My role model is Joni Mitchell, a totally inspired, creative, and self-assured woman. I also consider myself lucky to have had many wonderful personal friends and dedicated listeners. My No. 1 mentor when it comes to photography is my husband and business partner, Mark Sojdehee.

What business mistake have you made that you will not repeat?
Moving my home, renovating, and moving my business during the same two-month period!

Where is your favorite place to go with your girlfriends?
Out to dinner at an outdoor café, other than a journey to Peru!

PRÊT A POSER PHOTOGRAPHY

65 E Oak St, Chicago, 312.642.2211
pretaposer.com

Stylish. Artistic. Friendly.
Prêt a Poser Photography offers a creative, unobtrusive approach to capturing elegant contemporary portraits, as well as romantic candid images. Offering a variety of services to accommodate each client's specific needs—including destination weddings, family, and studio portraiture—Prêt a Poser's Gold Coast location provides the perfect opportunity for fabulous skyline and urban location shots.

PUMP SHOES & ACCESSORIES

1659 W Division St, Chicago, 773.384.6750
pumpshoeschicago.com

Feminine. Friendly. Fabulous.
A mecca for shoe addicts, Pump Shoes & Accessories showcases the crème de la crème at friendly prices. Fabulous flats, stunning stilettos, breath-taking boots, and all-day pumps fill this flirty shoe boutique. From frivolous to functional, Pump has something for every girl who's looking to sustain her fashion-plate status. Owner and buyer Maureen Longua Bueltmann ensures her boutique is always packed with unique footwear and trendsetting handbags, keeping Pump a stomping ground for urban sophisticates.

Q and A

Maureen Longua Bueltmann

People may be surprised to know...
I quit my job in marketing to sell shoes at
Marshall Field's so I could learn as much as
possible before I opened my shop.

What or who inspired you to start your business?
At the time I opened, Wicker Park was void of a fun,
feminine shoe store where a girl could take her shoes off
and play. So, six years later they are still coming to play.

Who is your role model or mentor?
My sister. She always told me I can do
anything I put my mind to, and supports me
all the way—even on the silly stuff!

What business mistake have you made
that you will not repeat?
Playing it too safe. Our gals count on Pump for fun
and fabulous. There's no room for boring feet here!

Where is your favorite place to go with your girlfriends?
I love any excuse to get dolled up and
go for cocktails with my girls.

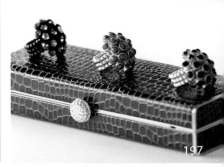

RANDOONS WEARABLES AND WHATNOTS

962 1/2 Green Bay Rd, Winnetka, 847.784.1890
randoons.com

Stylish. Charming. Enchanting.
Randoons is a hip clothing, accessory, and gift boutique bringing city style to the 'burbs. A couture café inspired by all things sweet and funky, Randoons offers everything from contemporary jeans and T-shirts,to luscious soaps and paper goods. Owner Randi Lamb's goal is to provide a unique and fun shopping environment—a place to buy that special gift or just get something you can't resist.

Randi Lamb

 Q and A

What are your most popular products or services?
Women's clothing, which is unique with great
price points. Also our handmade bakery soaps
and vintage-engraved serving pieces.

People may be surprised to know...
That I have my own line of women's clothing, a card
line, hand-painted ornaments, and a baby line.

Who is your role model or mentor?
My mother for always believing in me, and
my father for his endless creativity.

How do you spend your free time?
Eating out with family and friends, creating
something new, singing, playing guitar,
or just hanging out with my dogs.

Where is your favorite place to go with your girlfriends?
Antique hunting for displays for the shop,
shopping, and out to lunch. I love it!

RUBY ROOM—THE STYLE OF WELLNESS

1743-1745 W Division St, Chicago, 773.235.2323
rubyroom.com, Twitter: @RubyRoomChicago

Inspiring. Nurturing. Enchanting.
Ruby Room began as a healing sanctuary in 2002. Owner Kate Leydon's vision has unfolded over the years with the creation of a space that includes a salon, a spa, two distinctive boutiques, overnight guest rooms, a product line, and an e-store. Ruby Room's mission is to positively affect the energy and spirit of their clients by providing and recommending quality services and products that promote healing and beauty from the inside out. Some people call Ruby Room magical. They call themselves The Style of Wellness™.

Kate Leydon

Q and A

What are your most popular products or services?
Haircuts, Arcona facials, Intuitive Blend, Chakrassage, numerology, astrology, specialty workshops.

People may be surprised to know...
We have something for everyone in all price ranges.

What or who inspired you to start your business?
I wanted to leave a beauty mark on the face of the wellness industry through our commitment to healing, energy, and all things positive.

What business mistake have you made that you will not repeat?
Trying to do and be all things to all people.

How do you spend your free time?
Enjoying my family, practicing yoga, and resting.

What is your indulgence?
Dining out, crystals, jewelry, and purses.

Where is your favorite place to go with your girlfriends?
Janes Restaurant.

Nicci Lynne Plachno

 Q and A

People may be surprised to know...
I have worked in this industry since I was 15 years old.

What or who inspired you to start your business?
Myself, my daughter, my supportive family, and my
loving partner, Danny, who made it all possible.

Who is your role model or mentor?
James Tricoci for taking me under his wing
and teaching me exceptional skills, discipline,
professionalism, and passion toward my business.

How do you spend your free time?
Enjoying my beautiful backyard and pool
with my children, family, and friends.

What is your indulgence?
Traveling the world, designer purses,
and decorating my home.

Where is your favorite place to
go with your girlfriends?
A day at the spa or bike rides down Lake Shore Drive.

SALON 214 WEST

214 W Main St, St Charles, 630.443.9378

Sophisticated. Contemporary. Chic.
Salon 214 West is an award-winning, trendy salon in the heart of downtown St Charles. Owner Nicci Lynne Plachno and her team of stylists specialize in cutting-edge hair cuts and colors for the modern girl, and are known for their chic bridal up-dos. The salon also offers a line of custom-blended makeup.

What is your indulgence?

" *An uninterrupted afternoon alone with my sewing machine.* "

Jennifer Velarde, 1154 LILL STUDIO

Q and A

Sarah Levy

What are your most popular products or services?
Black-and-white cupcakes, chocolate-almond toffee, Chocolate Delights, and wedding cakes.

People may be surprised to know...
I still eat dessert every day. I don't think I will ever get sick of it!

What or who inspired you to start your business?
I am inspired by the joy that good food can bring to peoples' lives.

Who is your role model or mentor?
Chef Jacquy Pfeiffer for the pastry side; my dad for the business side.

What is your indulgence?
Chocolate chip cookies, toffee, chocolate croissants, and mac 'n' cheese. As far as non food-related: lip gloss.

Where is your favorite place to go with your girlfriends?
I love eating at Ron of Japan!

SARAH'S PASTRIES & CANDIES

70 E Oak St, Chicago, 312.664.6223
Macy's on State Street: 111 N State St, Chicago, 312.781.3004
sarahscandies.com

Delicious. Comfortable. Decadent.
Sarah's Pastries & Candies prides itself on consistently making outrageously delicious pastries and chocolates. Sarah's offers morning pastries, cakes, tarts, chocolates, cupcakes, wedding cakes, gelato and sorbet, gourmet sandwiches, Intelligentsia coffee and espresso drinks, and many more tantalizing treats. Owner Sarah Levy has worked at some of the country's leading bakeries and restaurants—including Spago Beverly Hills, as well as with pastry chefs Rafael Ornelas and Alexa Sindelar—since she started her company in March 2004.

SEQUOIA CENTER

30 N Michigan Ave, Ste 906, Chicago, 773.469.1507
kimberlysharky.com, Twitter: @kimberlysharky

Innovative. Dynamic. Individualized.
The Sequoia Center is a select group of professional therapists who specialize in couples therapy, and the confidential treatment of sexual concerns. Kimberly Sharky, founder of the Sequoia Center, is a licensed Marital & Family Therapist, as well as a licensed sex therapist. She and the professionals at Sequoia are dedicated to helping individuals and couples create the most vibrant relationships and lives possible.

Q and A

Kimberly Sharky

What are your most popular products or services?
The most sought after services at the Sequoia Center are confidential sex therapy and couples intensives.

People may be surprised to know...
I would love to be a travel and food writer as a second career!

What or who inspired you to start your business?
I was most inspired by my tireless, dedicated, and entrepreneurial mother; my first and most cherished role model.

How do you spend your free time?
Bikram yoga, training for half-marathons, cooking at home with my handsome man, and exploring undiscovered restaurants around the city.

What is your indulgence?
Only one?! I love a great bottle of Malbec, spontaneous travel, guacamole, and a massage followed by the steam room.

SKYEVENTS

Chicago, 847.529.6452
skyeventplanner.com, facebook.com/skyevents

Fresh. Distinctive. Passionate.
Offering personalized event planning services, SkyEvents is a distinctive company with a fresh, vibrant approach. Believing that class and style are unique to each individual, SkyEvents has a passion for exceptional client service. From weddings to galas to private parties, the goal at SkyEvents is to bring each client's unique vision to life, while staying true to both their taste and their budget.

Mila Sky

Q and A

People may be surprised to know...
My initial dream was to become an accomplished chef.

What or who inspired you to start your business?
After taking over the planning for a close friend's event, I realized that this was what I loved and was meant to do.

Who is your role model or mentor?
My mom. She taught me to be a strong woman, and to be able to stand on my own two feet, no matter what happens.

How do you spend your free time?
Hosting intimate backyard get-togethers for my close friends and family.

What is your indulgence?
A double bacon quarter pounder with cheese and large french fries... and a diet coke.

Where is your favorite place to go with your girlfriends?
Las Vegas!

Julie Smolyansky

Q and A

What are your most popular products or services?
Frozen Kefir with mochi and fresh fruit, Kefir smoothies with fresh fruit and superfood green powder, and Kefir parfaits with granola and fruit.

Who is your role model or mentor?
My mom, Ludmila. She opened her first European deli before she was 30, and then went on to open four additional stores with limited resources—all the while being the best mom in the world.

What business mistake have you made that you will not repeat?
Underestimating the amount of work operating retail locations involves.

How do you spend your free time?
Playing with my baby at the park, beach, or home.

What is your indulgence?
Getting a massage and going away for a weekend.

STARFRUIT

2142 N Halsted, Chicago, 773.868.4900
1745 W Division St, Chicago, 773.395.9300
Block 37
starfruitcafe.com, Twitter: @starfruitcafe

Bohemian. Stylish. Delicious.
The lighthearted lovechild of taste and nutrition, all probiotic Starfruit offers frozen kefir, kefir smoothies, and kefir parfaits. Good health and good vibes—all part of the Starfruit journey. Fro-yo will never be the same now that Starfruit has arrived.

Q and A

What are your most popular products or services?
Quiksilver, Original Penguin, Free People, Billabong, Reef, Element, O'Neill, and a few local designers.

Who is your role model or mentor?
I don't have a single role model. I admire bits and pieces of many people and try to add what I learn to my life and my business.

What business mistake have you made that you will not repeat?
I have made many mistakes that I probably could have bypassed if I would have just listened to my gut.

How do you spend your free time?
I go to the park for hours at a time with my baby, Scarlett, my dog, Cassidy, and my husband, Daniel.

Where is your favorite place to go with your girlfriends?
I love going to the Green City farmers' market to buy fresh produce, eat crêpes, and sit around in the grass... or hang out at a beer garden!

Carrie Ligman-Bowers

STELLAR26

4164 N Lincoln Ave, Chicago, 773.388.2626
stellar26.com

Stylish. Cool. Friendly.
Stellar26 is a clothing boutique for both men and women. Combining styles from West Coast cool and Colorado mountain chill with a splash of urban edge, Stellar26 is a simple, cool, laid-back place to shop.

SUSAN ELIZABETH DESIGNS

Chicago, 708.837.3577
susanelizabethdesigns.com

Adventurous. Versatile. Distinctive.
Susan Elizabeth's background in sculptural hollowware, an ancient and rarely practiced art form, strongly influences her design considerations as a jeweler. Creating jewelry using metalsmithing techniques such as forging, raising, piercing, and riveting, Susan is endlessly compelled to devise new structures. Her inventive style blurs the boundaries of artist and designer. Adventurous and bold, yet timeless, Susan Elizabeth's innovative jewelry appeals to everyone.

Susan Elizabeth

Q and A

What are your most popular products or services?
My earrings and rings always sell well, my necklaces are great for layering, and my cuffs are the eye-catchers.

What or who inspired you to start your business?
I worked at a boutique years ago while I was still pursuing my hollowware for grad school. Once the owners saw the jewelry I had made for myself, they wanted to place an order. They liked how my pieces stood out from other metal jewelry, and that gave me the confidence to continue growing and expanding my business.

How do you spend your free time?
Playing with my dog, Oliver, enjoying wine with friends, and relaxing with a good book.

What is your indulgence?
Anything chocolate! I love to bake—sweets are a weakness for me. I will always splurge on a great handbag as well.

SUSAN FREDMAN'S AT HOME IN THE CITY

350 W Erie, 1st Floor, Chicago, 312.587.8150
susanfredmanathome.com, Twitter: @jmaremont, facebook.com/SusanFredmanDesignGroup

Inspiring. Fresh. Stylish.
True luxury means giving yourself permission to explore your individual style. Susan Fredman's Chicago home store, At Home in the City, is peppered with everything one needs to create a lifestyle of luxury within an urban landscape. Her designers are on hand to assist customers in finding their "homes" desire. Not for the bashful or the weak at heart, it is a shopping experience that integrates turn-key design services and the absolute best of the best. Should you find yourself in Harbor Country, Susan's first retail location, At Home with Nature, boasts designer-selected products for retreat living.

What are your most popular products or services?
Interior design, bridal registry with a staff interior designer, home furnishings, and gifts.

How do you spend your free time?
In Harbor Country with my family and new puppy, Riley. I have had a second home in Harbor Country for more than 20 years and have a second interior design studio along with a home store in Union Pier, At Home with Nature. Harbor Country has its own vernacular, and families can relax and rejuvenate on the weekends.

People may be surprised to know...
Hiring an interior designer can actually help save money.

What or who inspired you to start your business?
My love of travel and my love of design.

Where is your favorite place to go with your girlfriends?
My retreat home in Harbor Country and travelling whenever possible. I love being immersed in different cultures, sharing meals and experiencing how people live in different countries with friends.

Susan Fredman

219

SWEET PAPIER

Chicago, 630.806.0240
sweetpapier.com, Twitter: @sweetpapier

Fresh. Charming. Sweet.
Sweet Papier is a charming little online "paper bakery" specializing in the scrumptious design of invitations, announcements, note cards, and party favors. They mix eco-friendly papers into their product line, and give back 10 percent of their earnings to organizations working to eradicate poverty around the globe.

Danette Zoda Yepsen

Q and A

What are your most popular products or services?
Invitations, chocolate bar wrappers, cupcake cartons, and note cards are the top sellers from our menu.

People may be surprised to know...
When they purchase our sweet paper products, they are helping to feed the hungry in parts of Africa and the Philippines.

What or who inspired you to start your business?
I wanted to model for my daughter that you should follow your heart and do what you love, even if it involves risk and uncertainty.

What business mistake have you made that you will not repeat?
Losing site of networking opportunities, and missing the opportunity to meet and learn from other small business owners.

Where is your favorite place to go with your girlfriends?
To the spa for beauty treatments, or out for coffee.

Q and A

People may be surprised to know...
Knitting is a creative art form which must be preserved. Because all our pieces are artisanal, creativity, innovation, and modern interpretations of knitting are essential elements in our brand.

Who is your role model or mentor?
My parents are my role models. My most recent mentor is Robert Zelvin, counselor for SCORE (SBA) Chicago.

What business mistake have you made that you will not repeat?
Funding a start-up with personal finances.

How do you spend your free time?
Reading industry research, surfing the Web.

What is your indulgence?
Shopping!

Where is your favorite place to go with your girlfriends?
When possible, exotic vacation destinations.

Sheri Jenkins (co-owner Tanya Henderson is not pictured)

TAHAJO

Chicago
tahajo.com, Twitter: @tahajo, facebook.com/tahajo

Versatile. Vibrant. Luxurious.
Tahajo is a modern luxury brand with the right mix of color, fashion, and signature styles. Offering luxury accessories suitable for weekends or for work. Tahajo accessories are sophisticated, unique accent pieces for both men and women. The product line includes hand- and machine-knit hats, scarves, neckties, shawls, ponchos, and handbags, which are carefully crafted to enhance personal style.

TANGERINE

1719 N Damen, Chicago, 773.772.0505
chicagotangerine.com

Entertaining. Lively. Cute.

In 1997, Tangerine opened its doors to Chicago. Fueled by an eagerness to learn the business and support her three daughters, Lori Mandarino turned a love of dressing women into a full time career. Lori's philosophy began and has remained simple, dress women so that they feel their best. Over a decade later, the philosophy has remained consistent, as well as the familial atmosphere. Don't be surprised to see the same team of women at Tangerine, as much of the staff has remained the same and has helped the store to continue to be a Bucktown favorite.

Lori Mandarino and Alex Averbach with their team

Q and A

What are your most popular products or services?
Although we carry several designers, our most popular lines are Tibi, Velvet, and Genetic Denim. We also carry a handful of exclusive lines.

People may be surprised to know...
Tangerine offers closet consultations and will be launching a clothing line in 2010.

Who is your role model or mentor?
I'm inspired by my daughters, my coworkers, and by people I meet everyday.

What business mistake have you made that you will not repeat?
Even eleven years later, I'm still learning everyday.

How do you spend your free time?
Hanging out with the women I'm closest with... my coworkers.

What is your indulgence?
Travel.

Tanya Hart

Q and A

What are your most popular products or services?
TOV is all about food and wine, and
both are offered in abundance.

People may be surprised to know...
We weren't even going to offer one on
the menu, but it turns out our burger is
probably one of the best... anywhere.

What or who inspired you to start your business?
Taking a career in wine for over 20 years
and turning it into my own business.

Who is your role model or mentor?
My grandfather. He was a chef and lover of good
food and wine. He always said, "do what you love."

What is your indulgence?
I love good pastries and fresh cream!

Where is your favorite place to
go with your girlfriends?
Out for great sushi and sake.

TASTE OF VINO

Taste of Vino - Wine Shop, Wine Bar and Bistro: 821 W Burlington Ave, Western Springs, 708.246.8668
Taste of Vino - Wine Shop and Wine Bar: 24 W Chicago Ave, Hinsdale, 630.325.8466
Taste of Vino - Wine Shop and Wine Bar: 27 Prospect, Clarendon Hills, 630.323.8444
atasteofvino.com

Innovative. Delicious. Stylish.
Taste of Vino (TOV) is Chicago-downtown-hip, in the 'burbs! Offering a unique, inexpensive wine and food concept, TOV not only has delicious food, but all the wine sold in the restaurant is priced at a retail rate, plus $12 corkage. There are three locations—two wine shop/wine bars, and one wine shop/wine bar & bistro—all located a mere 30 minutes from downtown Chicago.

TING DESIGNS

Chicago
tingdesigns.com, Twitter: @tingdesigns, facebook.com/tingdesigns.fan

Stylish. Creative. Practical.
Ting Designs offers a unique selection of chic and compact purse hangers to keep your beloved handbag off grimy floors and out of your lap. Each foldable hanger is exceptionally durable and will hold well over 15 pounds. Customizing your hooks will make memorable marketing giveaways or wedding favors. Ting Designs purse hooks can be found at restaurants, hair salons, and trendy boutiques.

 Q and A

People may be surprised to know...
Purse hooks have been around since the
1920s. They have evolved from a simple "S"
shape to foldable compact mirrors.

What or who inspired you to start your business?
One day, my girlfriend whipped out a traditional purse
hook during our Sunday brunch. It was love at first sight!

Who is your role model or mentor?
My parents are my role models. They work hard at
their businesses, which inspires me to do my best.

What business mistake have you made
that you will not repeat?
I used to be overly optimistic but now I always keep
a sliver of caution in case something goes wrong.

How do you spend your free time?
I love people! I spend a lot of time connecting with
people. It keeps me grounded and open minded.

Angela Lim

Tonya Mann

Q and A

What are your most popular products or services?
Most often I'm hired as a beauty expert to consult or write for clients. From the apron line, Tina and Beth are the most popular styles.

Who is your role model or mentor?
My grandmother was a beauty counselor and seamstress, with amazing style. She was my original role model.

What business mistake have you made that you will not repeat?
Trying to do everything myself. I thought if I asked for help, people would think I couldn't succeed on my own. As it turns out, that's not the case at all.

How do you spend your free time?
I love to travel, roam through antique stores, play with my puppy, and visit with family and friends.

What is your indulgence?
Lash extensions. I tried them when I was writing a magazine article and was instantly hooked. They make beauty easy and I love that!

TONYA MANN

Chicago, 616.406.8340
tonyamann.etsy.com, tonyamann.com, beautytipsy.blogspot.com, Twitter: @beautytipsy, facebook.com/beautytipsy

Playful. Pretty. Unique.
Former beauty editor and makeup artist Tonya Mann is in the business of beauty. Whether working with international beauty companies to help launch their latest products and brands; dishing on her beauty tipsy blog; or designing fabulous couture cocktail aprons and one-of-a-kind jewelry, her passion for helping women look and feel their best is evident in everything she does.

Rhodeshia
Nelson

Q and A

What are your most popular products or services?
We carry a staggering number of dresses from designers such as Diane von Furstenberg, Shoshanna, and Susana Monaco. From casual to cocktail, there's nothing more flattering, flirty, and feminine than a fabulous dress.

Who is your role model or mentor?
I am endlessly inspired by the female entrepreneurs I meet who are successfully balancing their business, family, and personal lives. I take every opportunity to learn what they have to teach.

What business mistake have you made that you will not repeat?
Like many entrepreneurs, I tried to squeeze 30 hours of work in a 24-hour-day. I had to learn the hard way to utilize the people and resources around me so I could truly focus on doing the work I love.

What is your indulgence?
Shoes. I have a separate closet just for my shoes, and I'm constantly adding to my collection. You can't have the perfect dress without the perfect pair of shoes.

TOTEM

35 S Washington St, 2nd Level, Hinsdale, 630.986.0900
shoptotem.com, Twitter: @shoptotem

Chic. Friendly. Trusted.
Totem offers a carefully edited collection of unique clothing and accessories for women and men.
In Totem's relaxed, welcoming atmosphere, classic pieces from fashion icons are seamlessly mixed
with edgier designs by up-and-coming labels. Their passionate stylists provide one-on-one service
and act as guides to our clients in building a wardrobe that makes them look and feel amazing.

233

TRIANON

1166 W Armitage Ave, Chicago, 773.880.8401
Twitter: @TrianonChi

Intimate. Experienced. Unique.
Providing the finest contemporary haircutting and color services, Pamela Orfanos and partner Edward Ebel have created seamless beauty as a color/cutting team for over 15 years. Together with their staff, they offer a unique and personable experience at this distinctively detailed Lincoln Park studio.

Pamela Orfanos

Q and A

What are your most popular products or services?
Our most popular service next to a haircut are highlights. They are easy to maintain, and colors can easily be changed to suit your mood, or the season.

Who is your role model or mentor?
My parents who are also business owners. They have always had a strong work ethic their whole lives, and they now have a lot to show for it.

How do you spend your free time?
Mostly with my son and husband. We lead a very busy lifestyle, so Sundays are sacred to us. We love to be at home together.

What is your indulgence?
A double espresso with cream on Sunday mornings, along with the *New York Times*.

Where is your favorite place to go with your girlfriends?
My girlfriends and I always have the very best moments at each other's homes. It's always comfortable.

TRIBECA

1035 W Madison St, Chicago, 312.492.9373
shopattribeca.com

Sassy. Sharp. Sophisticated.
Tribeca, the popular former Lincoln Park boutique has grown-up and moved to the hot
West Loop, where style is celebrated with a colorful and sharp edge. The focus is on unique,
yet wearable fashion, hand-picked by the owner in NYC and LA. You will spot independent
designers paired with tried-and-true favorites, with most items priced below $150.

Kim Hiley

Q and A

What are your most popular products or services?
"Going-out" tops, "date" dresses, premium
denim, handbags, and jewelry.

People may be surprised to know...
This is our 12th year In business!

What or who inspired you to start your business?
Sandy Horwitz, the owner of Clothes
Minded in Bucktown.

What business mistake have you made
that you will not repeat?
Having three stores open at once and not
spending enough time at all of them.

How do you spend your free time?
Cooking and strolling around the city.

What is your indulgence?
Fabulous restaurants.

ULTIMATE BRIDE

106 E Oak St, Chicago, 312.337.6300
ultimatebride.com

Stylish. Sophisticated. Professional.
Nestled on Chicago's prestigious Oak Street, Ultimate Bride continues its reign as one of the country's finest bridal salons. In this elegant setting, brides are surrounded by an amazing selection of designer gowns, and are given the undivided attention of an experienced stylist. From conservative to trendy, traditional to contemporary, Ultimate Bride is sure to have the perfect dress for your wedding day.

Q and A

Elena Grapsas

What are your most popular products or services?
Designer wedding gowns, personalized consultations, and superior alterations.

What or who inspired you to start your business?
My passion for beautiful gowns, and women looking their best.

What business mistake have you made that you will not repeat?
I have a tendency to overbuy at every market, and I promise myself each time not to make the same mistake.

How do you spend your free time?
I love traveling with my daughter and my husband. We often spend time in Europe enjoying the company of our friends and family there.

Where is your favorite place to go with your girlfriends?
NoMi at the Park Hyatt.

VICTORIA SDOUKOS COUTURE

924 W Madison St, Chicago, 312.226.9880
victoriasdoukoscouture.com

Chic. Glamorous. Innovative.
Victoria Sdoukos Couture, located in the West Loop, offers specialized, one-on-one private
consultations. During the appointment, brides receive a head-to-toe look by fashion designer
and owner Victoria Sdoukos, complete with custom-designed veil and jewelry.

Victoria Sdoukos

Q and A

What are your most popular products or services?
Giving the bride the opportunity to customize
every part of her wedding look.

Who is your role model or mentor?
My family. They have played a major role in my success
with their encouragement, talents, and wisdom.

**What business mistake have you made
that you will not repeat?**
Overworking and putting everyone else before myself.
I have since learned to balance my work and personal
life, and I accept that I cannot do it all in one day.

How do you spend your free time?
I really enjoy living in Chicago and exploring this
wonderful city. I'm inspired by music, art, and people.

Where is your favorite place to go with your girlfriends?
Tavern on Rush is a great place to
unwind and meet new people.

Kelly Proudfit

Q and A

People may be surprised to know...
We use all part-recycled papers. We also do search-engine optimization for Web site search results.

What or who inspired you to start your business?
I love design. I love paper, ribbon, and color.
I took my advertising background and used
it to build my home-based business.

What mistake have you made in your
business that you will not repeat?
Trying to do too much of everything. It's more
important to do just a few things well.

How do you spend your free time?
Outdoors with my 4-year-old son. I love gardening!

What is your indulgence?
Expensive shoes from JCREW, chocolate,
graphic design books.

Where is your favorite place to
go with your girlfriends?
Great restaurant with even better wine.

VISUAL AFFAIR & VISUAL VIEWS

Chicago, 412.352.9210
visualviews.com, visualaffair.net

Custom. Classic. One-of-a-kind.
Visual Affair offers custom, one-of-a-kind invitations. Wedding invitations, corporate events, baby showers, and birth announcements are their specialties. Visual Affair's goal is to make affordable custom invitations to fit your exact needs. Going green? They offer 100 percent recycled paper and soy-based inks. Need a Web site for your event? Check out their partner company Visual Views, specializing in Web solutions.

VIVE LA FEMME

2048 N Damen, Chicago, 773.772.7429
vivelafemme.com

Bodacious. Beautiful. Bitchin.
Vive la Femme is Chicago's premier boutique for stylish women of size! Offering the latest looks and trends exclusively in sizes 12-24, Vive la Femme has dressed thousands of curvaceously confident women since 2002. From retro to metro, work to weekend, ladylike to luscious, Vive la Femme is the go-to boutique for the full-figured fashionista.

Stephanie Sack

Q and A

What are your most popular products or services?
Our dresses are always flattering and foxy, and everyone loves our in-house line of handmade skirts.

What or who inspired you to start your business?
I am fat and I *love* clothes! I figured if I was fat and loved clothes, then other fatties loved clothes, too.

Who is your role model or mentor?
Betsey Johnson. Her vision is uniquely hers and has translated across decades and generations.

How do you spend your free time?
Taking Bikram yoga classes, road trips with my husband, and reading non-fiction.

What is your indulgence?
Shoes, jewelry, makeup, facials, massage, mani-pedis ... girly stuff.

Where is your favorite place to go with your girlfriends?
Out dancing!

Katrina Markoff

 Q and A

What are your most popular products or services?
Exotic Truffle collection, cheese and chocolate collection, Mo's Bacon Bar, Red Fire exotic candy bar, and the Groove collection.

People may be surprised to know...
I have my pilot's license.

What or who inspired you to start your business?
The Nagaland people of India.

Who is your role model or mentor?
My mom.

What business mistake have you made that you will not repeat?
Working with friends.

How do you spend your free time?
Riding my horses, planting seeds, and going everywhere with my sweet puppies.

What is your indulgence?
Chocolate!

VOSGES HAUT-CHOCOLAT

951 W Armitage, Chicago, 773.296.9866
520 N Michigan Ave, 2nd floor, Chicago, 312.644.9450
vosgeschocolate.com, Twitter: @Vosges

Experiential. Sustainable. Luxurious.
Vosges' exotic truffles are made from the finest ingredients from around the world. Owner and chocolatier Katrina Markoff personally chooses every spice, flower, and chocolate that is flown into her Chicago kitchen. Vosges Haut-Chocolat offers a luxury chocolate experience; a sensory journey bringing about awareness to indigenous cultures through the exploration of spices, herbs, roots, flowers, fruits, nuts, chocolate, and the obscure. Vosges invites you to explore the many cultures, artists, and theories of the world's people, through the medium of chocolate.

YOU JUST SHOP

130 Canal, Chicago, 312.523.9500
youjustshop.com, Twitter: @youjustshop

Friendly. Fun. Fabulous.
You Just Shop is Chicago's premier limo-driven, custom shopping excursion company, designed to deliver you and your friends to the doorsteps of the city's best boutiques. They've scoured Chicago to find hidden gems so your outing will feel like a treasure hunt. Whether you're tourists, brides-to-be, spa-goers, girlfriends, or families, You Just Shop has excursions just for you.

Q and A

Nancy Harris

What are your most popular products or services?
The most popular excursion is the Boutique Extravaganza, where guests are taken to the most stylish shops in chic neighborhoods.

What or who inspired you to start your business?
My love of shopping and fashion were the inspiration behind my business. I wanted to integrate fashion, fun, and friends.

Who is your role model or mentor?
My role models are my parents whose hard work, support, and love permeate everything I do and everything I am.

What business mistake have you made that you will not repeat?
Letting fear get in the way. Once the fear was released, I realized there was nothing to be afraid of.

How do you spend your free time?
Listening to music, practicing yoga, going shopping, traveling, and spending time with family and friends.

ZZP INC.

15623 S 70th Court, Orland Park, 708.269.7006
zuzuspetalsfloral.com, Twitter: @ZZPinc

Fresh. Beautiful. Sweet.
At ZZP Inc., excellent customer service, as well as your personal style, are at the center of each order fulfilled. With meticulous care given to each client's request, ZZP will ease your mind and relieve your stress, as they create the perfect floral setting for your special event.

Natalie Willett

Q and A

What are your most popular products or services?
Being an event florist, centerpieces
and bouquets are our specialty.

People may be surprised to know...
We are affordable and willing to work
within the client's budget.

What or who inspired you to start your business?
The movie "It's a Wonderful Life" inspired me to
help others and impart something beautiful.

Who is your role model or mentor?
My mom, of course!

How do you spend your free time?
Perusing flower Web sites, and writing.

What is your indulgence?
Red wine and candy.

Where is your favorite place to go with your girlfriends?
Good restaurants! Italian, Asian, whatever!

251

Intelligentsia Directory

Business-to-Business entreprenesses, including
coaching, marketing and public relations, photography,
business consulting, and design services.

AUDIENCE

Chicago, 773.244.2336
audienceengages.com, Twitter: @laplax

Results-driven. Flexible. Affordable.
Specializing in small- to mid-sized businesses, Audience is all about creating
and developing marketing and PR strategies that make a positive impact on
your bottom line and connect you even more to your "audience."

L.A. Plax

Q and A

What are your most popular products or services?
Budget-conscious marketing and PR strategies.
Launching social media campaigns. Special-
event planning and promotion.

People may be surprised to know...
The Audience team focuses on internal
marketing, too! A business' employees
can be the best marketing resource.

What or who inspired you to start your business?
My children. I wanted/needed a more flexible
schedule. As the previous VP of North America for
a research company, I was traveling like crazy.

How do you spend your free time?
I love time with children and hanging out
with friends! Happy hour is fun, too!

BABY SWAGS

PO Box 1233, Plainfield, 815.342.6739
babyswags.com, Twitter: @babyswags, facebook.com/BabyswagsPR

Successful. Unique. Trusted.
Baby Swags is a celebrity gifting company that reaches out to new celebrity moms and their babies. Baby Swags specializes in promoting maternity and juvenile-related products that have been created or invented by mom entrepreneurs.

Phyllis Pometta

What are your most popular products or services?
Celebrity gifting, press releases, product placement, VIP gift bags, and gift suite production.

What or who inspired you to start your business?
I started Baby Swags after I had my own product-based business. I attended a gift suite and came home with an idea to help mom entrepreneurs get their products in the hands of celebrities at a much lower cost, while still producing the same results.

How do you spend your free time?
Whatever free time I have, I spend with my children. I have three who are all very different, so I try to do something special with each of them. As for mommy time, I enjoy spending hours at the bookstore thumbing through design or cookbooks.

CALLIOPE DESIGN

Chicago, 773.457.2761
calliopedesign.weebly.com

Vibrant. Creative. Intuitive.
Calliope Design, from conception to connection, is a design boutique. With experience developing results-driven design for print and Web, Calliope Design is the solution for your organization's graphic-design needs. Like all successful artists, we have a tireless muse, which brings joy to our work and shines through in the final product.

Caryn Mitchell

Q and A

What or who inspired you to start your business?
To follow my bliss! And, all the other beautiful people who love what they do and are joyful! The world is a better place for it!

Who is your role model or mentor?
My Aunt Gretchen who shared her wisdom and insights, and lived her life to the fullest with ease, joy, and comfort.

People may be surprised to know...
I create mosaic art and designs that beautify peoples' environments.

What is your indulgence?
Getting a massage!

Where is your favorite place to go with your girlfriends?
When we're together, it doesn't matter where we are!

CHICAGONISTA

Chicago, 312.213.6471
chicagonista.com, Twitter: @mjtam

Creative. Involved. Informative.
Chicagonista—"movers, shakers, and baby makers"—is an online magazine that provides the buzz about Chicago's diverse spots and events, unearthing both hidden city gems and long-forgotten city favorites.

MJ Tam

 Q and A

How do you spend your free time?
I enjoy running around the city with my three kids in tow. If I'm by myself, I run to the nearest bookstore, and, indulging in all the free hands and time I have, I hunt for new books to inhale.

What or who inspired you to start your business?
Chicago inspires me! Just when I thought I'd seen everything I wanted to see in my 20s, my eyes and ears are more open now that I'm in my 40s. And with three new little sets of eyes to explore with me, I have lots of material to blab about in Chicagonista.

What business mistake have you made that you will not repeat?
Trying to do everything myself. I've learned to delegate better and trust that things will go right if I take more time training the right people.

EMILY DEWAN PHOTOGRAPHY

Chicago, 773.502.0795
www.emilydewan.com, emilydewan.blogspot.com, Twitter: @emilydewan, facebook.com/emilydewan

Creative. Captivating. Friendly.
Photographer Emily DeWan captures memorable images, creating art out of ordinary experiences. Her friendly spirit and nature allow her to connect with people of all ages, and allows them to feel completely at ease in front of her lens. Her unobtrusive style of shooting leads to artistically captured memories for her clientele. Emily is available for weddings, events, and portraits.

Q and A

Emily DeWan

What are your most popular products or services?
Wedding photography coverage and portrait sessions.

What or who inspired you to start your business?
My very first photography teacher in high school.

What business mistake have you made that you will not repeat?
Trying to be too many things at once. Not everyone is your client!

How do you spend your free time?
Swing dancing (around town and around the country) and singing (with my barbershop chorus).

What is your indulgence?
Homemade cookies—especially the batter!

EXPECT MARKETING SUCCESS, INC.

Chicago, 312.375.2979
expectsuccessnow.com

Small Business Coach.
Expect Marketing Success (EMS) helps you focus on what you know best: your business.
Whether you are just starting out and need a winning plan encountering serious business
roadblocks to further your success, or are already successful and want to become more
so, EMS can help. Their motto: We help entrepreneurs turn their passion into profit.

Vera Michelle Lewis

Q and A

What are your most popular products or services?
Developing strategic marketing plans, teaching
clients how to reach their target audience,
and helping clients acquire new customers
and keep existing customers active.

People may be surprised to know...
If you are a woman considering small business
ownership, this is a perfect time for you. Don't
let lack of money or expertise stand in your way.
Have confidence in your valuable life experience,
and draw from it when starting your business.

Who is your role model or mentor?
My father, who started his own business back
in the '60s. He was an innovative African-
American man who was ahead of his time. He
is my role model and mentor to this day.

GINA CRISTINE PHOTOGRAPHY

Chicago, 708.516.4677
GinaCristinePhotography.Com, Twitter: @GinaCristine, facebook.com/GinaCristinePhotography

Artistic. Natural. Fresh.
Gina Believes in focusing on your newborn/child/children/family in a artistic, fun, natural, and fresh way. She will come to your home or location of your choice and uses only the natural lighting available. She captures and documents your family's personality so it will be frozen in time forever.

Gina Cristine Sandrzyk

What are your most popular products or services?
Full photography sessions at clients homes.

People may be surprised to know...
I was a competitive figure skater!

What or who inspired you to start your business?
My daughter, Ava Grayce.

What business mistake have you made that you will not repeat?
Not backing up my contact list.

How do you spend your free time?
Relaxing with my husband and daughter.

Where is your favorite place to go with your girlfriends?
Out for sushi and martinis.

HADELROCK CAPITAL MANAGEMENT LLC

125 N Marion St, Ste 206, Oak Park, 708.386.9100
hadelrock.com

Trusted. Consistent. Results-driven.
Hadelrock is a leading Chicago-area alternative investment management firm focusing on fundamental event-driven absolute return strategies. Client returns are generated by investing in short-term equity and option arbitrage opportunities caused by corporate event, economic environment, or market mispricing. Hadelrock's experienced investment team has been successful in delivering positive returns throughout the economic cycle, with low correlation to traditional asset classes.

Q and A

Joan Rockey

People may be surprised to know...
I am the chairman of the CFA Society of Chicago, a 3,700 member financial organization and the world's sixth-largest CFA Society.

What or who inspired you to start your business?
Being able to make a difference. Of the 9,000 worldwide hedge funds, only 100 are owned by women or minorities.

Who is your role model or mentor?
My hard-working, generous parents, Lawrence and Conchitta Grabowski. They taught their kids they could do anything.

How do you spend your free time?
Long-distance running, cooking, volunteering for numerous non-profit organizations, and playing with my beautiful daughters, Ellery and Hadley.

JACKIE CUYVERS

Chicago
jackiecuyvers.com, Twitter: @jackiecuyvers, facebook.com/jackiecuyvers

Creative. Innovative. Synergic.
As a full-service, online marketing and digital media guru, Jackie Cuyvers uses strategy, implementation, and education to help her clients increase sales, generate buzz online, and establish brand advocates offline. Services include online marketing, social media strategy, digital publicity, and online reputation management.

Jackie Cuyvers

What are your most popular products or services?
Digital publicity, online reputation management, online marketing, and social media strategy.

People may be surprised to know...
Even if you're not actively promoting your brand online, someone else is already talking about you.

What or who inspired you to start your business?
I come from an entrepreneurial family with a love for technology. Having seen a need for helping women entrepreneurs successfully market themselves online, it seemed like a natural fit.

What business mistake have you made that you will not repeat?
Don't move to a new office too soon. Use what you've got for as long as you can.

JULIA SHELL PUBLIC RELATIONS

Chicago, 312.203.3130
juliashellpr.com, Twitter: @juliashell, facebook.com/juliashell

Non-stop. Tricky. Entertaining.
Julia Shell Public Relations has been providing public relations services since 1999. With a concentration in "lifestyles" publicity, focusing on events and entertainment, including dining, nightlife, music, fashion, health, fitness and sports. From product launches to grand openings to fundraisers—for Fortune 500 companies or mom-and-pop shops—Julia Shell Public Relations has got it covered.

Julia Shell

What are your most popular products or services?
I only have one product: publicity! Everybody wants it for their business, and I help them achieve it.

What or who inspired you to start your business?
My first client, Bally Total Fitness. They asked me to consult rather than hire me, so I started my business and it's been growing ever since.

How do you spend your free time?
Balanced between my wonderful kids, good friends, cool clients, and gratifying volunteer work. Oh, and sleeping.

What is your indulgence?
Guinness, Vosges Chocolate, Dave Chappelle, and the Flight of the Conchords.

JULIE DARLING, INC.

Chicago, 312.217.0380
juliedarling.com, Twitter: @julieanndarling, facebook.com/julie.ann.darling

Customized. Unprecedented. Memorable.
Julie Darling is a full-scale event marketer who specializes in lifestyle and luxury. Julie firmly believes in forming strong, personal bonds with her clients by producing dazzling events and providing unparalleled public relations services. From concept to completion, Julie Darling understands her clients, and, as a marketing professional, she is resolute in exceeding their wildest expectations.

Julie Darling

 Q and A

What are your most popular products or services?
Event marketing and full-scale public relations.

People may be surprised to know...
I'm an avid animal lover, but my favorite is my lovely Lola, a 120-pound Landseer Newfoundland. She really is a showgirl!

What or who inspired you to start your business?
From a very early age I watched my mother follow a career in real estate sales. I was raised to be very independent and learned to always be happy. Inner happiness is what allows me to continue to move forward.

How do you spend your free time?
Dinners with friends, cooking with loved ones, playing with Lola, listening to live music, and reading the latest from the *New York Times* Best Seller List.

KARLENE M. ANDERSON

Chicago
kolesuk.tripod.com/karlenemanderson, Twitter: @karleneanderson, facebook.com/karlene.anderson

Creative. Detailed. Affordable.
Karlene M. Anderson's entrepreneurial project marketing and PR consulting business began while she was at college. Integrating experience with corporations, non-profits, small businesses, and individuals, Karlene M. Anderson understands research, policy, administration, development, communication, and online social networking, with clients in the Chicago area and beyond.

Karlene Anderson

Q and A

What are your most popular products or services?
Writing web content, grants, news releases, and radio and television spots; editing Web content and radio and television spots; database management, and customer service.

What or who inspired you to start your business?
I was inspired to start my own business by people asking me to help them accomplish their projects or goals. Also, my father inspired me because he started his own business, Olesuk Financial Services, in McHenry.

How do you spend your free time?
My husband and I like to travel, watch movies, take walks, or hang out with friends and family. I play musical instruments, too.

What is your indulgence?
Ice cream and sleeping late (when I can).

KITTY SINGSUWAN DESIGN

Chicago, 312.637.9669
kittysingsuwan.com, Twitter: @kittysingsuwan

Stylish. Talented. Focused.
Kitty had high hopes for advertising, until someone wanted a brochure. Soon, the projects rolled in, and Kitty Singsuwan Design is what you see today—a full-service graphic design studio, specializing in logos, packaging, and Web sites. Known for their keen sense of style and balance, and for the ability to convey messages with clarity and impact, Kitty Singsuwan Design creates beautiful designs, so their clients can promote themselves beautifully.

Kitty Singsuwan

Q and A

What are your most popular products or services?
Logos, packaging, and Web sites.

What or who inspired you to start your business?
I actually fell into my business. I was looking for a job as an art director when someone wanted a brochure. The projects have been flowing ever since.

How do you spend your free time?
I love to run, soak up the occasional art exhibit, and ogle modern architecture.

What is your indulgence?
Handbags.

Where is your favorite place to go with your girlfriends?
I love meeting up with my gal pals for dinner. Wherever. Whenever.

THE LAW OFFICE OF MEAGHAN L. SCHNEIDER

Chicago, 312.371.2800
mls-esq.com

Energetic. Creative. Diligent.
Meaghan is a solo practitioner in Chicago delivering customized legal solutions to her clients. She counsels small- and mid-sized companies, guides solopreneurs, and represents established business owners. She writes and reviews business plans, operating agreements, sales contracts, leases, and employment terms, among other papers, and has worked with clients on their marketing, licensing, and risk management issues.

Meaghan L. Schneider

Q and A

What are your most popular products or services?
Good businesses are built on good contracts. I work with my clients to create iron-clad contracts.

People may be surprised to know...
I was an heiress to a Greek island.

Who is your role model or mentor?
My parents taught and modeled good values that have carried me through most of what I've done in my life.

What business mistake have you made that you will not repeat?
I undervalued my time and work product, until I realized that a one-woman firm can deliver five-star service.

How do you spend your free time?
I enjoy spending time with my family and on a sunny weekend morning, hitting the links for a round of golf.

LIDIA VARESCO DESIGN

Chicago, 773.777.8517
lsvdesign.com, Twitter: @lsvdesign

Enthusiastic. Imaginative. Dedicated.
Lidia Varesco Design is a boutique graphic design studio with a passion for the finer details that make each product shine. Their decade-long success lies in their imaginative approach, obsession for detail, and exceptional communication. In addition to design and marketing services, Lidia Varesco Design also offers their own line of greeting cards and stationery, found in local shops and online.

Lidia Varesco

Q and A

What are your most popular products or services?
For my design clients, logo/branding and marketing materials. With my stationery customers, occasion-specific greeting card sets are popular.

People may be surprised to know...
I speak three languages. (Though they may get a hint when they see my Italian greeting cards!)

What business mistake have you made that you will not repeat?
Taking on too much work without being prepared. Now I make sure my team of fellow designers is on stand-by.

How do you spend your free time?
Traveling, reading, sketching, practicing yoga, enjoying life with family and friends—preferably outdoors when the Chicago weather cooperates.

LIGHT ON LIFE IMAGES

Chicago, 773-456-4024
lightonlifeimages.com, Twitter: @lightonlife, facebook.com/kristi.k.sanford

Friendly. Professional. Relaxed.
Kristi Sanford shoots in a documentary style to chronicle the distinctive story of your wedding, event, or family life. Although Light on Life photographs formal and impromptu portraits, Kristi works hard to capture key moments as they unfold. Additionally, Light on Life specializes in documentary photography for non-profit organizations committed to social justice and the common good.

Kristi Sanford

Q and A

What are your most popular products or services?
Documentary-style wedding photography, custom designed wedding albums, and on-location family photography.

People may be surprised to know...
I speak fluent Spanish, having studied abroad in Argentina via a Rotary Scholarship after high school. I'm a travel junkie—I've visited a dozen countries. My favorite vacations were hiking the Inca Trail in Machu Picchu, Peru, and backpacking in New Zealand. I hope to get to Italy and India soon.

How do you spend your free time?
When I'm not looking at other artists' photography, I enjoy practicing yoga, biking, and cooking with vegetables from the local community-supported agricultural organic farm.

Featured Crave Photographer

LOVE-L, INC.

Chicago, 773.235.2685
love-l.com, Twitter: @michelekravetz, facebook.com/lovelinc

Dynamic. High-energy. Efficient.
Love-L, Inc. was formed with business owners in-mind. Understanding there is not a lot of extra time in your day-to-day life to invest in social media facilitation, Michele Kravetz is here to offer a solution! She works behind the scenes providing low-cost and fabulous social media interaction and simple event coordination. Love-L wants to serve you and help business owners find a little more "me" time.

Michele Kravetz

 Q and A

What are your most popular products or services?
Social media is so right-now; every package I offer is in high demand!

What or who inspired you to start your business?
Too many business owners were asking me how to make the most of their tweeting, blogging and facebooking. I thought, I can help them do this!

What business mistake have you made that you will not repeat?
Jumping into an idea too quickly may result in unforeseen challenges. I recommend sleeping on every decision that must be made!

How do you spend your free time?
Enjoying my love's marvelously prepared meals at home or dining at our city's amazing selection of restaurants!

MERCURY ORGANIZING PROFESSIONALS

Chicago, 312.804.2111
mop-ds.com

Competent. Effective. Refreshing.
Mercury Organizing Professionals are efficiency experts. By creating innovative organizing systems, they help clients eliminate obstacles and minimize distractions, thereby saving them time and money, and reducing their anxiety and frustration levels. In both home and office settings, Mercury Organizing Professionals are masters at space utilization, allowing their clients to function at their absolute best.

Q and A

What or who inspired you to start your business?
I recently discovered that I am a good motivator, and that I have the ability to help people become more successful by changing their organizing habits.

Who is your role model or mentor?
My mother has been a strong influence in my life and is my role model. Her dedication to service has been instilled in me as well.

How do you spend your free time?
I enjoy cooking and spending time with my family and friends.

What is your indulgence?
Chocolate!

Where is your favorite place to go with your girlfriends?
Going to museums or festivals, or listening to live music.

Elizabeth Lulu Miranda

MORGAN MELTO PHOTOGRAPHY

Chicago, 312.970.9386
morganmelto.com

Bold. Passionate. Awesome.
Morgan Melto Photography buzzes with life, creating images that leap off the page. From fantastic food, to loving couples, to gorgeous spaces, to new products, Morgan's practiced eye for unique, quirky, attractive, and just plain fun guarantees photos that are anything but ordinary.

Morgan Melto

 Q and A

What are your most popular products or services?
Food photography, engagement and family portraits, and graphic design services.

People may be surprised to know...
I love to cook, photograph, and eat delicious vegetarian food, then blog about it at morgandotcom.com.

How do you spend your free time?
Bikram yoga—I have to counteract all the eating somehow.

What is your indulgence?
Cookies, coffee, and ice-cold wine— not necessarily in that order.

Where is your favorite place to go with your girlfriends?
There is nothing better than chatting with girlfriends over wine and cheese flights.

OLSON COMMUNICATIONS, INC.

Chicago
olsoncom.com

Intuitive. Quirky. Unconventional.
Offering innovative communication strategy for the food industry since 1988, Olson Communications takes pride in the personal connection they make with clients across the globe. With their uniquely creative and intelligent approach to marketing, Olson Communications has gained international recognition by remaining small, while exceeding the range and depth of service typically offered by larger food-marketing agencies.

Sharon Olson

Q and A

What are your most popular products or services?
Culinary inspiration for non-culinary professionals. Both our Culinary Visions Panel and our Culinary Boot Camp for business executives get rave reviews.

People may be surprised to know...
How inspired, creative, and flamboyant someone gets when the suit jacket comes off and the chef's jacket and toque go on—it's amazing!

What or who inspired you to start your business?
I was in a business known for burn-out. I wanted to prove that you could have fun, make money, and make a difference.

Who is your role model or mentor?
My husband, Fred. I think he stays up nights thinking of ways to bolster my confidence and make me feel amazing.

PIVOTAL PRODUCTION

Chicago, 773.983.6328
pivotalchicago.com, Twitter: @PivotalChicago, facebook.com/PivotalProduction

Sassy. Client-centric. Unique.
Pivotal Production is a full-service event company focused on creating engaging experiences, fabulous events, and titillating spectacles. This boutique firm not only has the resources and creative gusto to manifest anything their clients can dream up, but they're environmentally and socially responsible as well!

Shannon Downey

People may be surprised to know...
Green events do *not* have to mean more money, and they certainly do *not* mean burlap and incense. Pivotal works hard everyday to find creative alternatives to traditionally wasteful event practices, without affecting the look, feel, or price of your event. You want haute, whimsy, flirty, dramatic, edgy? You got it!

Who is your role model or mentor?
My role models are the amazing women business owners in Chicago who support me, challenge me, teach me, and, remind me everyday of the power of collaboration. I am constantly humbled by the brilliance of the company that I am fortunate to keep.

Where is your favorite place to go with your girlfriends?
Anywhere with good food, good art, good music, and Guinness on tap!

ROBYN RACHEL PHOTOGRAPHY

Chicago, 312.451.6389
RobynRachelPhotography.com, Twitter: @RobynRachel

Organic. Artistic. Timeless.
Robyn Rachel Photography is organic photography that captures naturally occurring moments and freezes them in time for families to enjoy as heirlooms. Robyn Rachel specializes in high fashion wedding photography, artistic children's portraits, and authentic family and high school senior sessions. She believes that photography should be organic, vibrant, and timeless, not over-posed and forced.

Robyn Rachel Lindemann

Q and A

What are your most popular products or services?
High-fashion weddings, as well as creative, one-of-a-kind children's portraits.

People may be surprised to know...
I am a green photographer and consider my style of photography "organic."

What or who inspired you to start your business?
From the first photo I took, my Uncle Dave believed that I had a gift and pushed me to turn a passion into my career.

How do you spend your free time?
Working out, watching sports, baking, and spending time with my family, friends, and pets.

What is your indulgence?
Traveling the world.

TASTY CMS

Chicago
tastycms.com, Twitter: @tastycms

Creative. Friendly. Accessible.
Tasty CMS offers an economic, creative solution for Web site management that allows businesses and individuals to edit, add/delete, and upload photos—without the need for a designer or Web developer. For clients who already have a Web site, Tasty CMS can easily transfer the existing site to their easy-to-use system. Best of all, their hours are flexible to work around your schedule!

Amy Knittel

 *Q and A*

What are your most popular products or services?
Our Content Management System, Tasty CMS.

What or who inspired you to start your business?
I wanted to help new, small businesses create an online presence by providing quality and affordable Web site solutions.

Who is your role model or mentor?
My husband, Ed, is a born entrepreneur, and he inspires me with his passion, wealth of knowledge, and creative thinking.

What business mistake have you made that you will not repeat?
At first I didn't attend many networking events, but I soon realized meeting someone in person is more powerful than a friendly phone call or e-mail.

TAXLINK, INC.

4051 N Damen Ave, Chicago, 773.549.5100
taxlinkinc.com

Warm. Upbeat. Inviting.
Taxlink, Inc. specializes in income tax preparation and consulting for individuals and small-businesses, offering affordable, professional, high-quality service, in a relaxed and inviting atmosphere. Through personalized service and attention to detail, Taxlink strives to develop lasting relationships with their clients, so they will return year after year with confidence.

Elizabeth Stock

Q and A

What are your most popular products or services?
Tax preparation and business consulting.

People may be surprised to know...
I like to climb mountains.

What or who inspired you to start your business?
Being an entrepreneur runs in my family. We are very driven.

Who is your role model or mentor?
I tend to admire women who are strong and self-sufficient.

How do you spend your free time?
Traveling with my husband, shooting photography, or hanging out with my dog.

TWO K PRODUCTIONS

Naperville, 630.518.6947
fashionweeknaperville.com, Twitter: @fashionweeknape

Energetic. Dynamic. Unforgettable.
Two K Productions is a fashion event planning company specializing in upscale events for designers, retailers, restaurants, and charitable organizations. Both Kristen and Kristy are former models and draw from their experiences on and off the runway to deliver unforgettable fashion based events.

Kristen Frederick and Kristy Brezinsky

What are your most popular products or services?
Fashion event planning and fashion show production.

People may be surprised to know...
That we don't crumble easily! We're very nice, but effective and tenacious too.

What or who inspired you to start your business?
We were inspired by our friendship, common backgrounds, and our daughters. Together we wanted to do what we love and still be able to be home for our little girls.

How do you spend your free time?
With our families and our daughters!

Where is your favorite place to go with your girlfriends?
We both love sunshine, an outdoor patio, and cocktails.

ZOKA ZOLA
ARCHITECTURE + URBAN DESIGN

1737 W Ohio St, Chicago, 312.491.9431
zokazola.com

Sustainable. Multifaceted. Innovative.
Zoka Zola and her team of designers believe that space is capable of influencing our ever-changing daily lives. This core belief is evident in their inclusive method to architectural design. Synthesizing the multitude of influxes on a project—client needs and ideas, budget, site location, regulations, urban and social context, sustainability, available technology, and building methods—Zoka and her team translate these intricacies into innovative, award-winning design.

Zoka Zola

Q and A

What are your most popular products or services?
What our clients value most is our approach to design. Personally, I'm way more interested in architecture than myself, so I don't see design as an opportunity to push my self-expression. Rather, our team acts as a medium for clients—always listening first, then channeling and synthesizing ideas to create new and unique experiences.

What or who inspired you to start your business?
I started off wanting to be a physicist. It was my sister who was studying to become the architect. I remember her recounting the conversations she was having at university. I realized that through architecture I could still grapple with the big, important issues of our universe, only in a way that felt more vital, more real to me.

Photographic Contributors

BJORN KAVANAUGH
Chicago, 312.846.6253, bjornphoto.com

Nostalgic. Easy going. Creative.
Bjorn's work fuses small-town warmth and sincerity with an urban, photojournalistic aesthetic, for a sense of ease, integrity, and nostalgia in every image. Bjorn studied photography at Andrews University, where he curated gallery and multimedia events. He is strongly influenced by the work of Sebastian Salgado and Henri Cartier-Bresson, as well as by his own background in architecture and design.

JON SHAFT
Chicago, 734.788.5548, jonshaft.com

Fashion. Editorial. Lifestyle.
Jon Shaft is a photographer working in Chicago. His fashion and editorial photographs have appeared in publications such as *Chicago Social (CS)* and *New City Magazine*. The focus of his work is on the human subject, but his portfolio also includes architecture, food, and travel. Jon's work is highly influenced by cinema, literature, fine art, and by everyday experiences.

PAMELA LUEDEKE PHOTOGRAPHY
Chicago, 773.319.2188, pamelaluedeke.com

Fashion Forward Photojournalism.
Pamela Luedeke is a wedding, fashion, and band photographer who focuses on capturing real moments in time, with a fashionable twist. She credits the success of her work to seeing uniqueness in every client, capturing the special energy that makes them who they are, resulting in photographs that convey both an image and emotion.

A Guide to our Index

Manifest by category

Manifest by category

Manifest by category

Manifest by neighborhood

Manifest by neighborhood

Manifest by neighborhood

$\mathcal{M}$anifest by neighborhood

$\mathcal{M}$anifest Intelligentsia Directory

the
CRAVE company™

Innovative Connections

The CRAVEcompany innovatively connects small business owners with the customers they crave. We bring together small business communities and fuel them with entrepreneurial know-how and fresh ideas—from business consulting to shopping fairs to new media. The CRAVEcompany knows what it takes to thrive in the modern marketplace. thecravecompany.com

CRAVEparty®
What do You Crave?

CRAVEparty is an exclusive, festive, glam-gal gathering of fun, entertainment, personal pampering, specialty shopping, sippin' and noshin', and just hanging with the girls.

CRAVEguides™
Style and Substance. Delivered.

CRAVEguides is the go-to resource for urban-minded women. We celebrate stylish entrepreneurs by showcasing the gutsiest, most creative and interesting proprietors from cities all over the world.

CRAVEbusiness™
A Fresh Approach to Modern Business

CRAVEbusiness is a social, resource network for stylish innovators who own their own business, or dream of starting one. Through one-on-one consulting, workshops and red-carpet access to sage and savvy experts, entrepreneurs meet with others in their fields to get a fresh approach to their business.

Craving Savings

Get the savings you crave with the following participating entreprenesses—one time only!

10 percent off

- [ ] @WorkDesign
- [ ] À Pied
- [ ] About Face Cosmetics
- [ ] Adele Dallas Orr pret a porter boutique
- [ ] The Bleeding Heart Bakery
- [ ] Bramble
- [ ] Brynn Capella
- [ ] Camp Bow Wow McHenry
- [ ] Chocolate Gourmet (online only with code CRAVE)
- [ ] Embellish Boutique
- [ ] Engaging Events by Ali, Inc
- [ ] Essential Blueprints (online only with code CRAVE)
- [ ] Eye Want
- [ ] G Boutique
- [ ] GAVIN Evanston
- [ ] The Gold Hatpin
- [ ] Gray Wellness (online only with code CRAVE)
- [ ] Honey
- [ ] Karen Zambos (online only with code CRAVE)
- [ ] Karlene M. Anderson
- [ ] Kickin'
- [ ] Kitty Singsuwan Design
- [ ] Koros
- [ ] Ladysmith Jewelry Studio (online only with code CRAVE)
- [ ] Lauren Lein Design
- [ ] Le Dress
- [ ] Light on Life Images

10 percent off (continued)

- [ ] Mercury Organizing Professionals
- [ ] Mulberry & Me
- [ ] One Mind Body & Being
- [ ] Prêt a Poser Photography
- [ ] Smash Cake
- [ ] Susan Fredman's At Home in the City
- [ ] Sweet Papier (online only with code CRAVE)
- [ ] Tahajo (online only with code CRAVE)
- [ ] Take the Cake (online only with code CRAVE)
- [ ] Taste of Vino
- [ ] Tasty CMS
- [ ] Ting Designs
- [ ] Tribeca
- [ ] Victoria Sdoukos Couture

15 percent off

- [ ] 1154 LILL STUDIO
- [ ] Barker & Meowsky, A Paw Firm
- [ ] Baubo's Garden
- [ ] Bellybum Boutique
- [ ] Chicago Kids Bookstore and More
- [ ] Colori Eco Paint Boutique
- [ ] five ACCESSORIES (online only with code CRAVE)
- [ ] Fredda ID
- [ ] Harmony Haus
- [ ] Hunny Boutique
- [ ] Kee2Creativity (online only with code CRAVE)

Craving Savings

15 percent off (continued)
- ☐ Love, Lulu Mae (online only with code CRAVE)
- ☐ The Meatloaf Bakery
- ☐ Mudd Fleur
- ☐ Name your design (online only with code CRAVE)
- ☐ Peek-a-Boutique
- ☐ Pump Shoes & Accessories
- ☐ Randoons Wearables and Whatnots
- ☐ Stellar26
- ☐ Trianon
- ☐ Vive la Femme
- ☐ You Just Shop

20 percent off
- ☐ Aniko Salon and Spa
- ☐ Anjénu
- ☐ Audience
- ☐ Chocolate For Your Body Spa
- ☐ Fly Bird
- ☐ Genacelli Salon
- ☐ Gina Cristine Photography
- ☐ Harmony Mind Body Fitness
- ☐ Isabella Fine Lingerie
- ☐ Julie Darling Inc.
- ☐ Knickers of Glen Ellyn
- ☐ Lisa Rosen Jewelry (online only with code CRAVE)
- ☐ Morgan Melto Photography
- ☐ Noteworthy
- ☐ Olive Owl Organics

20 percent off (continued)
- ☐ Pair Chocolates
- ☐ Sequoia Center
- ☐ Totem

30 percent off
- ☐ Colette Salon and Spa
- ☐ Susan Elizabeth Designs (online only with code CRAVE)

50 percent off
- ☐ Starfruit